LIMITLESS GROWTH

A CONTINUOUS PURSUIT FOR GREATNESS

JOHNNY L. FRANKLIN JR.

Limitless Growth: A Continuous Pursuit For Greatness

johnny.lee.franklin@gmail.com

Elite Publishing Press

Library of Congress Cataloging-in-Publication Data is available upon request.

ISBN 978-1-7336321-0-2

Ebook ISBN 978-1-7336321-1-9

Manufactured in the United States of America

Table of Contents

ENLARGE YOUR VISION 1

KNOW YOUR SELF-WORTH.......................................10

ACCEPT THE CHALLENGE 20

ATTITUDE IS EVERYTHING 27

FALL IN LOVE WITH HARD WORK 38

KEEP YOUR EYES ON THE PRIZE 48

KEEP PRESSING FORWARD 57

THE COMPANY YOU KEEP 67

APPETITE FOR SUCCESS 76

EXTREME MAKEOVER 85

UNDERDOG STATUS 93

OWN YOUR GREATNESS 100

LIMITLESS GROWTH 109

ENLARGE YOUR VISION

The life that you have is something quite special and unique. Your life is something that can be viewed as a great opportunity to do monumental things that will leave behind a legacy. Have you ever taken time to think about the great things you're capable of accomplishing during your lifetime? Some of us may currently be in a state of having a diminished vision of what we could possibly create with our lives. Having a diminished vision hinders us from being great and living life to the fullest. Life has no limits, unless you create those limits upon your own. If you're a person that has a small or diminished vision about life, it's now time for you to enlarge your vision and change your life for the best. Open your mind and heart to accept nothing short of pure greatness. You were destined to be great, but you won't be able to capture that greatness with a small vision on life. You're absolutely capable of accomplishing anything. Take it upon yourself to have courage and believe in your abilities. When you believe in yourself, nothing can stop you. Broaden your view on life because you have unfinished business to handle.

The way that other individuals picture how your life should be doesn't matter. It simply doesn't matter because other individuals are not the ones walking in your shoes every single day. You're in total control of your life and you dictate your own success. Other people in this world are not the ones going to work or school for you on the regular basis. In our society today, there are so many people who are overly concerned with how others view them. More so, there are many people who take into consideration other individual's opinion regarding their own capabilities and how they should live their lives. It's a well-known fact that not every person you come in contact with during your lifetime will have your best interest at heart. Everyone is not your friend and there are some people who don't want to see you succeed in life. Often times, you may experience coming in contact with people who try to purposely poison your mind with negative expectations about your life. When situations like this occur, your job is to believe the opposite. You can't expect for someone else's view about your potential to succeed to be bigger and brighter than your own view. There are some people in this world who do want to see you succeed and reach your greatest potential, but this could be a very small crowd of people as well. The most important view of your life comes from your own eyes and what you choose to believe. You run the show and you must never forget that.

Depending on where you are in life or what circumstances you encounter in life, these could be the determining factors of how easy or hard it would be for you to enlarge your vision about your life. For example, an individual's socioeconomic status plays a big role in how they may view their potential to succeed in life. Your socioeconomic status can be measured as a combination of your income, education, and occupation. As a child, if you grew up in a household where your parents had very little education and earned an income that was below the national poverty level at that particular time, the thought or dream of being able to one day obtain more than what your parents were able to earn may have never crossed your mind. The reason behind that could be because of your lack of exposure to more experiences and the information about life that you were receiving from your parents. If you had parents who really struggled and believed that their life conditions couldn't get any better, you were exposed to that mindset of small vision. People with a small vision pertaining to life opportunities have little hope and sometimes believe that there's nothing better for them in the future. Children have the ability to absorb things they hear and the actions they see from their parents like a sponge. Parents play the most important and influential role of a child's early development of learning. Growing up or living in an environment of poverty could possibly make a person believe that there isn't more to life outside of their dark shell of existence. An environment of poverty can be dark, dangerous, and gloomy. Those who live in poverty may view their environment as a rainstorm that will never pass or subside. Many children grow up with this outlook on life and continue to live with this mindset into adulthood. It's important that all adults, regardless of their circumstances in life, preach hope and opportunity for more success into the lives of the young. For those who grew up in a family where education was cherished and there was no struggle in the area of income, you can understand and witness that life has limitless opportunities to succeed and grow. Unfortunately, everyone doesn't get to experience this type of upbringing in their lifetime. If you were raised in a family where education was highly praised and you didn't have to worry about money, your eyes were opened to view the world as a place of great opportunity.

If the existence of having a small vision about life is being passed down from generation to generation by a family, this cycle can be broken. It may take a great amount of work and effort, but it can definitely happen. Having small vision isn't a permanent registered mindset that can't be corrected. It's always best to believe that anything is possible. Collectively, a certain group of people could come together and break a cycle. Sometimes, it only takes one person to step up and break a trending cycle. If the determination and effort is in place to make the correction, things are bound to transform into positive results. If the existence of having a small vision about life is being passed down from generation to generation in your family, make the decision to stop the cycle right now. It's better to stop the cycle now rather than let it continue to destroy your entire family. Your entire life depends on it. You're too great of an individual to have a small vision about life. You were meant to do extraordinary things and help other people in this walk of life. If you're a parent, you definitely don't want your children to think that there's not much they can accomplish in their lifetime. If you have children, you surely want to see them blossom like a beautiful flower in a garden. If you're a parent, plant seeds of hope, courage, determination, and broad vision into the hearts and minds of your children. If you have children, give them an opportunity to understand and believe that nothing is impossible.

One major reason why you should enlarge your vision about life is because there's so much opportunity available for you in this world. Every single day that you wake up with another chance to live, you must aggressively run after present opportunities like it's the last twenty-four hours of your life that you'll ever see. Every single day that you wake up, hit the pavement and get busy living. If you fail to see potential or opportunity that's available in your life, you definitely need to change your focus and take a second look at your life. There's so much more available for you than what you currently see. If you have a lack of faith and confidence in your ability to achieve more than where you currently reside, you'll be unable to see upcoming future opportunities. When your vision on life is small, there could possibly be an opportunity staring you right in your face and you would miss it as if you were blind. Having a small vision about life places barriers and blockage against greatness that's just patiently waiting for you. During your lifetime, some opportunities that become available to you will only come around once. That's just how life operates sometimes. If you don't enlarge your vision about life and what you're capable of doing, there are opportunities in life that will pass you by and move on to other people. This complete concept about life is mind-blowing and definitely true. When you fail to act and reach out to take advantage of an opportunity, you intentionally allow a blessing to pass you by. Taking advantage of precious opportunities can change your life forever. Enlarge your vision to grasp opportunities that may only come available to you once in your lifetime.

Enlarge your vision to give yourself the opportunity to do phenomenal things in life. When you enlarge your vision about life, it not only helps you propel yourself into the realm of greatness, but it also gives other people a sense of confidence to make their own dreams come true. You can easily become a role model and example for other individuals. When you believe that anything is possible and other people witness your belief, that energy alone can be contagious and set a fire inside of others. This is the type of contagious energy that needs to be passed down from generation to generation in every single family. In regards to the work industry and work environments, the contagious energy flow of optimism must be present for agencies and companies to be successful. This is the type of energy that you want around you on a consistent basis. You have the ability to pass this contagious energy to your friends, associates, co-workers, and even strangers. Along with making the honest effort of enlarging your vision on life, don't be afraid to push others to do the same. Encourage other people to believe in ideas or actions that they may think is impossible. Some people are unable to enlarge their vision because of what they currently see with their eyes in their present situation. Challenge others to become optimistic and direct their focus beyond any current state or situation. A lot of people need help with this and they'll greatly appreciate you challenging them to be better. Every single individual that walk this earth should make sure that helping others is at the top of their list of life goals. Choosing to enlarge your vision about life will open doors not only for you, but it will make room for others as well. Keep your mind and heart open for growth and advancement. When you enlarge your vision, there's absolutely nothing that can hold you back from achieving more.

Every single day that you open your eyes, make it a must to not take the opportunities that life presents to you for granted. You won't live forever on this earth. Live every day of your life in a respectful and grateful manner as if it was your last day on earth. Treat every great opportunity as if time won't allow another opportunity to unfold during your existence. Go after what you want and don't place any limits on what you can achieve. Strongholds can make it extremely difficult for you to enlarge your vision on life. Strongholds will only exist in your life if you allow them to be present. There's nothing that can hold you back from greatness. The only person that has the ability to hold you back from being phenomenal is yourself. Wake up every morning with a sense of hunger for victory in every aspect of your life. Visualize how your life will continue to grow every single day. Take time out of your busy schedule to just think about your future. For most adults, we're doing so many things every day and we hardly ever take aside time to focus on ourselves, blocking out all of the noise from the world. If you visualize and believe that you have more goals and dreams to conquer in the future, that visualization will eventually unfold into reality.

KNOW YOUR SELF-WORTH

One of the most significant things in life that you should be aware of and thoroughly understand is your self-worth. Knowing and understanding your self-worth is just as valuable as the air you breathe. For your benefit, it's a must that you have a clear understanding of your level of importance. Understanding and knowing your self-worth could be the determining factor in the amount of success you're able to obtain during your lifetime. If you want to succeed in accomplishing the goals you've set for your life, along with making lifelong dreams come into existence, it's a necessity that you recognize your self-worth. Other people that you come across in your lifetime may also have the ability to recognize your self-worth as well, more so in a positive way. These individuals could be people that are close to you such as your parents, teachers, friends, or family members. These particular individuals could have the ability to see greatness within you and the potential you have to do more in life. In all, it's good for other people to acknowledge your greatness and potential, but it's not as equally important as how you determine your own self-worth. If you don't know your self-worth and what you're capable of accomplishing, your life will sadly go to waste. You'll miss out on blessings and opportunities that are meant for you. Know your self-worth and set the tone for how you choose to live your life.

As you travel through your journey of life, it's extremely important that you believe and have great confidence in yourself. You must be confident in your abilities and always believe that you have what it takes to overcome obstacles in your life. On many occasions, some people in this world we live in may misjudge confidence as cockiness. For a person who has a low level of confidence or absolutely no confidence in their abilities at all, this type of person could easily misjudge someone's confidence as cockiness. A person that's cocky can be described as being overly self-confident in an aggressive way, showing an offensive attitude of being superior over others. These types of individuals will often have a hard time being excepted by other people. People that are confident truly believe in themselves, showing a high level of self-worth. Confidence and cockiness is clearly not a reflecting mirror image of each other. Confidence and cockiness are two totally different things. To the untrained eye and lack of general understanding of these two totally different words, you or anyone else could be unable to distinguish one from the other. When it comes to your relationships with others or the lines of communication you have with other people, you never want to misjudge those individual's actions of confidence as cockiness. This would possibly create a barrier that would prevent the development of a good relationship or line of communication with another person. Know the difference between confidence and cockiness for your own sake and for the sake of your relationships with others.

There's absolutely nothing wrong with being a confident person. Everyone in this world should display the action of being confident on a consistent basis. The world we live in thrives off confidence. Having confidence is one of the critical keys to success. People that are confident have the ability to attract positivity and make room for great things to unravel in their lives. What type of energy or actions do you attract in your life? It's a well-known fact that the way you think and operate determines what you attract. Everything in your life initially starts with you. If you decide to go through life with a low level of confidence, you'll miss out on so many great opportunities. It would be almost as if you were wearing a special kind of blind fold throughout life that only blocked out things or opportunities you didn't believe were meant for you. Opportunities would be looking you right in the face and you wouldn't even see them. This is a very terrible way to live everyday life. Many people wake up every single day and are living this type of detrimental lifestyle. If you want more out of life, you must be confident. When you're confident, you put yourself in position to obtain greatness. Greatness doesn't come to those who have little faith and are afraid to dream big. Choose to chase your dreams every day of your life and don't look back over your shoulder. Today is your day to be great and you must claim it. Be confident in your abilities and you'll see your life evolve into something beautiful.

When you show a low level of self-esteem and others are able to witness it, you open the door of opportunity for other people to take advantage of you. In this world we live in, some people make it their duty to seek out others who are weak for their own beneficial achievements. These types of people are always hungry for new prey on a regular basis. Just as career criminals that exist in our society today, many people make it a lifestyle to seek out people with low self-esteem. Unfortunately, some individuals are brought up and taught at a young age that taking advantage of people is one way to get ahead in life. This type of lifestyle may possibly get you ahead in life, but you'll eventually have to pay for all your negative and intentional actions toward others. Many people are taught that this is the only way to achieve success and maintain it indefinitely. That's definitely not true. This is a learned behavior and action that totally goes against true moral behavior. If this type of behavior correlates with how you choose to treat other people, you need to drop this bad behavior immediately. In our society, rather than taking advantage of other people, we should be helping and caring for one another. We should be making a daily effort to motivate and assist other people when we're able to. Behaving in this type of manner will make you feel good about yourself. Showing love to other people will always feel better than taking advantage of them. Miserably, we all have to be cautious of other people in our society that don't practice good moral and ethical behavior. The snakes in our communities are out and busy looking for individuals they can sink their fangs into.

In our society, there are a great number of women who are being taken advantage of by men on the daily basis. Some of these women are the victims of verbal, physical, and emotional abuse. As a positive contribution to our society, there are still a great number of men who are actually great significant others or husbands. We need more men like this that can be a good role model for our younger generation of males growing up. We don't want our younger generation of males to grow up thinking that there's nothing wrong with taking advantage of women. There are quite a few men in this world that search and seek for women with low self-esteem that they can take advantage of at a low cost. These particular men have a way of thinking that involves exploiting women for their own personal benefit. It's easy for some women to fall into the traps of bad men because these men initially disguise their true colors and motives. Once the true motive is discovered by some women, they immediately get out of the situation. In many cases, it may take a substantial amount of time for some women to actually discover a vicious man's motive before they finally free themselves from the situation. Sadly to say, there are too many women who never exit the stronghold of a man who repeatedly takes advantage of them on the regular basis. Being taken advantage of is no form of love at all. Love doesn't bring you heartache and pain. Love is designed to make you feel happy and bring you a great sense of comfort. The brainwashing by unmoral men has damaged the lives of many women in this world. Vicious men are definitely out to seek their prey.

If you're a woman who's suffering from the malicious stronghold of an unmoral man, take a stand against his malicious ways of taking advantage of you and placing a damper on your greatness. It's not destined for you to be treated like you're worth absolutely nothing. You're too precious to be taken advantage of by the hands of anyone. All women are meant to be respected and treated with great kindness. Being brutally mistreated and taken for granted is an unfortunate situation that so many women have experienced. If you're a woman who's suffering from the hands of an unmoral man and you knowingly allow it to continue to take place in your life, understand that your self-worth is not being honored by that particular man. Take back the power and control of how you choose to live your life. Break free from those who cause you harm and start back enjoying life. Only you can determine the direction of your life. Life isn't worth living in misery and heartache forever. Living that type of life is like living a slow painful death. Everyone has the ability to pick themselves up and change their life around when it's not going in the right direction. If you're a woman who's experiencing this kind of situation with a disrespectful man, recognize your true self-worth and begin to make the proper adjustments to get your life back on a positive track. All women are precious queens that deserve love and peace.

One of the most important golden standards in life is that you must have genuine love for yourself. When you love yourself, you're able to prosper and enjoy life. If you don't love yourself, some people will take advantage of you if they feel that they can be successful at doing so. Also, if you don't love yourself, you may not possess the ability to properly show love to others. The way you think about yourself will dictate certain things that transpire in your life. When you have a low level of self-worth about yourself and think that your life is not as important as other human beings, you're heading down a road of destruction. Your life is just as important as anyone else that walks this earth. Even if there are people who are in a better condition financially or possess more authority than you in the community, your life is still as equally important as their lives. In our society, people have been misguided to embrace the concept that more money and authority than other people means greater importance amongst others. This concept about life is definitely not true. Never live by or believe this fake concept about life. This is a misrepresentation of how to measure the value of a person's life. There are a lot of concepts about life that have been preached by many people in this world who truly don't understand the value of a human life. A human life is precious and should never be taken for granted. Know your self-worth by truly understanding that your life is important and your existence carriers a heavy weight of greatness.

Each and every single person on this earth was designed to fulfil a specific purpose. If you're alive, there's a specific mission set out for you to accomplish before your time is up on this earth. To be specially crafted and molded into a living force with its own uniqueness, that alone should allow you to recognize or understand your value of existence. If your existence carries a great abundance of positive weight, why let someone else or people strip and break down your greatness? You're absolutely bigger than that. You have the ability to do many phenomenal things as you walk this earth. You're a giant that's meant to conquer and not be bothered by small meaningless things. Every day that you roam this earth, make your presence known. Send out vibes to the world that your greatness will make a lasting impact on the world forever. Even after you die, your greatness will always be remembered. Lift your head high and believe that greatness is upon you. Don't fall into the trap of others who are striving to take advantage of your gifts, talents, blessings, and love. If you leave the door open for people to strip you of your greatness, be looking forward to a living room full of company. Predators are always lurking to seek out the weak and feeble. Leaving the door open to be stripped of your greatness allows uninvited house guests to invade your privacy and take over.

The value and overall cost of your life is priceless. There's absolutely no dollar amount that would be equivalent to how much your life is worth. Even materialistic items could never measure up to a human life. You must take it upon yourself to uphold your self-worth to its highest standard of importance. Your life is meant to be in the same conversation with greatness because you are great. If you uphold your self-worth to its highest standard of importance, there's nothing in this world that can stop you from being phenomenal. Choose to have great confidence in all of your skills and abilities. There's nothing too great or powerful that can hold you back. When you're phenomenal, you shine just as bright as a star in the midnight hour. As a phenomenal individual, you soar above the clouds like an eagle in the sky. Even in a storm, you can soar above the clouds to an altitude that allows you to dodge the rain. You were specially crafted by the creator so always choose to live up to greatness. When you think about how important oxygen is to your existence, compare that to the importance of knowing your self-worth. If you're not able to breathe, you'll surely die. If you don't know your self-worth, your opportunity to display your greatness will die.

ACCEPT THE CHALLENGE

E xperiencing challenges is simply a normal part of life for all humans. Challenges come in many different forms and can present themselves at unexpected moments. On some occasions, we have the opportunity to see challenges before they actually begin to play an active role in changing our lives. When challenges present themselves, we all have two options to choose from when deciding how to handle them. We can either face them head on or choose to quit and run away from them if possible. The way you choose to handle a challenge that presents itself in your life will dictate how your future will turn out. Your choice will ultimately affect your life forever. There are many people living today who are experiencing the repercussions of quitting or running away from a challenge they experienced in their past. When certain situations are not properly handled, they can have an everlasting effect on us and can ruin our lives. The only way that you can prevent something of this magnitude from placing a damper on your life is to accept challenges. Whenever a challenge presents itself to you, it's in the best interest of your future to decide to accept it. Take challenges head on even if they seem hard to overcome. Refusing to accept challenges will prevent you from being great and phenomenal. Choose to stand tall because you're bigger than any challenge that comes your way. Standing tall against challenges now will prepare you for future battles. Toughness and confidence is built when you fight your way through battles. Accept challenges and welcome them with open arms into your life.

One of the most beautiful things about challenges is that you receive something great in return after your challenge has been ultimately defeated. On the other side of challenges, there are rewards to be claimed. These rewards are available for anyone to obtain. In sports, professional athletes compete amongst each other through the challenging elements of their particular sport. At the end of battling and facing the challenges of competing, every sport rewards their best players and teams with a trophy. In comparison to sports, when you stand up and win the battle against challenging circumstances in life, you'll receive a reward in the end. That reward symbolizes your success and your effort of winning against the odds if there were any that existed. Have you ever been in a situation where you felt that the odds against you were greater than your ability to achieve success? A situation like this can be a bit uncomfortable, but your uncomfortableness shouldn't block your focus of the reward at the end of the finish line. Get acquainted with being uncomfortable if you want to achieve success and prosper in life. Rewards will never come easy. With great confidence and determination, accept the challenges that come your way and fight hard until you have no more to give.

Some rewards are so glamorous that they tend to have an everlasting effect on our entire lives. Pursuing and furthering your education does have a major impact on your life. College students get their share of challenges to battle while they're in school. For many college students, certain college curriculums can be very hard and difficult to pass. Sometimes, students may have to put in an excessive amount of hours to study and complete assignments. At the end of conquering the challenges of college life, students are greatly rewarded with their degrees or certifications. Those degrees and certifications also open doors for career opportunities. Besides education, there are many other things that have an everlasting effect on our lives. Regardless of whatever challenges you face in life, remember that a reward is waiting for you at the end of those challenges. In order to receive a reward, you must fight and compete with every single ounce of determination that you have in your body. If you're trying to get in good health, attempting to start a business, working toward getting into a certain career field, battling an addiction, battling against depression, or encountering financial struggle, you must stand strong and fight. Fight and wrestle with your challenges to ultimately declare victory. You're a champion and victory patiently awaits you. You have what it takes to be victorious so begin to act like it every day of your life.

One thing that challenges can do in our lives is force us to come out of our comfort zones. In many cases, some people choose to settle and may never bother to take a step beyond their comfort zone. Your comfort zone is simply a world within the actual world we all live in. Falling in love with your comfort zone can be detrimental to your overall existence as a human being. For one, refusing to step outside of your comfort zone will hinder you from exploring or experiencing other opportunities in life. If you never step outside of your comfort zone and take on a challenge, how would you ever know what you're capable of accomplishing? How would you ever unleash the potential greatness that you solely possess? For example, many of us have great ideas on developing new things that may have never been done by mankind. The world is always open to great ideas and inventions that serve a purpose of making the world a better place. Also, we all have dreams and goals that we ultimately want to accomplish during our lifetime. The only way that we can make our dreams and goals become a reality is by accepting challenges and putting in the work that's required to be successful. If you never choose to step outside of your comfort zone, you'll never experience greatness that's well within your reach. Greatness can surely be achieved by anyone who's willing to work hard for it.

In addition to falling in love with your comfort zone, refusing to step outside of your comfort zone and take on a challenge may possibly leave you in a situation that's harmful to you. Believe it or not, challenges may arrive in our lives to actually save us from future harm. For example, let's say that your family has a history of diabetes. The cause of diabetes in your family could be because of poor diet and lack of exercise. In your life, you may feel that exercising regularly and eating specific foods is a big challenge. As a determining factor of your future existence, if you choose to not exercise regularly and eat healthier, you risk becoming diabetic and could cut your years of living short. Making the decision to take on the challenge of exercising regularly and eating healthier would actually save your life. Why not choose to take on the challenge? In a way, not taking on the challenge gives off the impression that you don't care about how long you're going to live. Your life is very precious and any challenge is worth facing to help extend your time on this earth. Step out of your comfort zone and take on challenges that arrive in your life. Don't be afraid to step out of your comfort zone to even look for and pursue challenges. Never have the mindset that your comfort zone will always be a safe place from danger.

Throughout our lives, challenges will allow us to grow and also prepare us for future challenges down the road. This is another valid reason why we should gladly embrace challenges that come our way. Encountering challenges is something that you'll be repeatedly faced with in this journey called life. Once you pass the test and conquer a challenge that has made its presence in your life, be expecting for another challenge to arrive soon on your doorstep. Challenges are simply an opportunity for growth. Continuous growth is needed to survive in the world and to improve our overall personal development. As you continue to live day by day and get older over the years, you should want to always grow in wisdom and intelligence. Being the same person with the same mindset throughout your entire life will get you absolutely nowhere. Without continuous growth, you'll fall well short of greatness. We all make mistakes, but only a fool continues to bump their head over and over again from the same mistake. One important part of growing is learning from your mistakes and making the proper adjustments to help you avoid making similar mistakes in the future. If the world is steadily changing and evolving on a continuous basis, why would you choose to not evolve as a person? Choosing to take on challenges for promoting personal self-growth will build your character and make you stronger for future battles in life.

When challenges arrive in your life, make a bold decision to accept them. Even when certain challenges seem as if they're impossible to conquer, step out on faith and meet them head on. You're phenomenal and phenomenal people have the ability to be victorious no matter how high they have to climb to conquer challenges. If you're able to see a challenge heading your way before it even touches down to make your acquaintance, simply begin to smile. You should smile because an opportunity for self-growth is on its way. For those individuals who love to improve their skills, talents, knowledge, and abilities, they get a pleasure out of being met with challenges. For some people, going out to seek challenges is a natural part of life. If you really want to experience greatness, you have to go out and get it because it won't fall into your lap. If you're seriously hungry for improvement, you'll do whatever is necessary in order for you to achieve improvement.

ATTITUDE IS EVERYTHING

The way that we approach life situations plays an important role in results and outcomes. A person's attitude is the foundation of creating a personal perspective, which is followed by actions that are thought to be for the best. Your way of thinking and feelings should be directly in sync with positivity and confidence. In regards to the situations you encounter in your lifetime, you have absolute power over deciding and choosing how you'll respond. Within your inner arena of personal perspective, it's definitely possible that you can allow outside sources, such as other people, to be disruptive or have an influence on how you choose to act or feel. What type of attitude do you display in the midst of challenges, new surroundings, or just change in general? When certain situations occur in your life, your attitude within those situations can either allow things to potentially move in your favor or make the situations difficult for you to thrive. Even during the course of challenging moments, choosing to have a positive attitude in the midst of your storms can grant you a sense of peace and satisfaction. On several occasions, some people choose to blame others for their inability to thrive or accomplish goals. If you're not accomplishing your goals, being presented with good opportunities, or thriving in developing positive relationships with other people, it may be your attitude and overall approach to life that's hindering you. Choose to have the attitude of a conqueror and champion. Have an attitude that allows you to take advantage of certain opportunities in life that will help you grow. Don't have an attitude that will close doors, preventing you from obtaining greatness. Your attitude is an important part of your legacy that will be left behind when you're gone away from this world. Your attitude is everything.

The type of attitude that you display to other people or during certain situations says a lot about you as a person. A person's attitude speaks volumes in regards to their true personal character. How do you want other people to view and distinguish your personal character? When you're in the presence of other people, your attitude will always be used as a source for judging or distinguishing the type of person you are as a whole. This is one reason why you should always strive to display your best at all times. In our society, most people generally state that first impressions are extremely important for the purpose of judging one's personal character. For job interview purposes, your first impression can greatly assist you with obtaining a job successfully or place you at the bottom of the list of eligible candidates. When people have short conversations with you and determine their personal opinion regarding the type of person you are, they begin to decide how they'll continue to deal with you during future interactions. If you want to develop good relationships with people that cross your path, you must have a genuine and positive attitude. Negative attitudes give off bad vibes, which will most likely make other people not want to associate themselves with you. Would you want to hold relationships with people who have terrible attitudes? Always choose to present your best and do it with a great attitude. Greatness is impossible to achieve when your attitude isn't up to part.

For those individuals who are in leadership positions in work environments, your attitude within your work environment is accountable for the progress of work being completed, the direction that your company or agency is heading, the atmosphere of the work environment, and the type of relationships you have with people who work with you. The attitude of a leader plays a huge role in the working industry. The success or failure of companies, agencies, organizations, and groups fall heavily on the leadership that's guiding everything. If you're in a leadership position and you currently don't have the right attitude to properly operate a business or agency, you should strongly consider changing your attitude very quickly. Not changing your attitude quickly will continue to destroy opportunities of progress for your business or agency. Having a bad attitude for business will label you as a dysfunctional businessperson. Ultimately, not changing your attitude will get you removed from your leadership position permanently or continue to destroy your company, giving it a bad reputation for business. Choose to be a leader that has a great attitude for leading a business or agency. Be positive, confident, and show passion for what you do. Show those individuals you lead that you take your work very serious. If you're not serious about the work that you do, the people that work with you won't take you serious at all.

If you're a leader, you must have an attitude that will allow you to develop good relationships with the people you work with on the regular basis. When your attitude is categorized or identified as dysfunctional, your relationships with others won't thrive and grow. Continuous growth within the relationships you develop with people is important. For the leaders in today's work industry, in order to experience the growth and positive development of relationships with others, you must have an attitude that expresses togetherness. To accomplish this, you must show others that you honestly care about their thoughts, opinions, and feelings. This will definitely help bring togetherness into existence. If unity cannot be established among a group of people, be prepared for failure to be lurking around the corner. Failure will strike and inflict a painful blow when you place yourself in a position to be hit. When the togetherness factor is in full effect, greatness will blossom as a result of the unity that's been accomplished. As a leader, demonstrate an attitude of loyalty toward the people you rely on to assist you with getting work and goals accomplished. Being a leader can be a difficult task, but it can definitely be done with the proper mindset and attitude. When you're in a leadership position, having the wrong type of attitude will make your job even more difficult, on top of the challenging obstacles that already exists within leadership. Attitude is one of the most important driving forces for achieving success. Success is up for grabs for anyone to embrace. Have the right attitude in order to achieve greatness that's well within your reach.

Having the proper attitude during difficult situations gives us the ability to focus our attention mainly on the positive aspects of the challenges at hand. In life, we all encounter our share of hard times and challenges. That's a natural part of life. During these hard times and challenges, our attitude has a major impact on how the situation itself will affect us while going through the process. For example, let's say you're currently working at a job that you absolutely dislike. On most mornings, you dread getting out of the bed to go work for this company, agency, or organization. On some occasions, you may even call in sick to work, even though you're really not sick. Some of the things that you don't like about the job could be the salary, the work schedule, bad management by those in leadership positions, or the way certain co-workers behave at work. Even though working at this job brings about certain challenges and dislikes, other bright aspects of the job still exist. In the midst of any challenge or difficulty, you can still discover some positive light. The only way that you would be able to see the positive aspects of this job, even though there's so much chaos in the atmosphere, is if you focus your attention directly on the positive.

One positive aspect of working at this particular job is having the opportunity to even be blessed with a job. In our society, there are so many people who are unemployed and struggling to survive day by day. The number of people that are homeless and living on the streets is continuing to grow. If you currently have a job, you've been blessed with a grand opportunity to make money so you can support yourself and your family. Secondly, working at this job you so greatly dislike is still helping you build your resume and gain experience, which will strongly benefit you in acquiring future employment.

While taking the bumps and bruises when working in a bad work environment, give yourself credit for it on your resume. Any work experience or training you receive on your job should never go undocumented for the sake of your future. Also, while working at that job you dislike, keep in mind and have confidence that the job you dislike is not going to be your final job. That job you so heavily dislike is just a temporary stopping point on your journey to success. Don't allow that job to bring you down and break your spirit. More employment opportunities are available for you to explore. Can you see how this kind of thinking can help you weather the storm of a bad job? Choose to have the right attitude during unpleasant and challenging situations. Having the proper attitude opens your eyes to focus on the positive. Furthermore, having the right attitude allows you to obtain a level of peace in the midst of any situation. As long as you have the proper attitude during your storms, you can survive.

When you go through life with the right attitude, you create the opportunity to attract positive things. In reality, we all are bound to encounter situations in life that we would rather choose to not be a part of, but our attitudes can also place us in positions that are more favorable to our liking if we play our cards right. From a social standpoint, people with great attitudes and personalities can easily connect with other individuals. People are more open to other individuals that they feel are good genuine people. When you have a negative attitude or personality, you'll most likely be unable to make many friends. It's really not that important to have hundreds and thousands of friends, but it's hard for anyone to honestly consider you as a potential friend if your attitude and overall personality isn't up to part. When your attitude isn't in connection with positivity, the friends that you do have and the people you affiliate yourself with will most likely be a reflection of your dysfunctional personality. If you want to truly create good relationships with other people and attract people who really have a good heart, you must display the characteristics of a person who has a positive attitude. The law of attraction is definitely real and very powerful. Use it wisely with the right attitude and make great connections with other people in the world.

From an opportunity standpoint, having the right attitude will open doors for you. Regardless of the mass number of terrible employers that currently exist in the work industry, there are still good businesses and companies in the world that offer great employment opportunities. Some businesses and companies that exist make it their duty to create a work atmosphere that's comfortable for their employees, along with promising opportunities for growth within the workplace. If you're currently employed with a business, company, or agency that demonstrates this kind of business excellence, your work ethic and attitude will determine how far you'll be able to go within your place of employment. When you have the right attitude in your work environment, opportunities for advancement and promotions will become available to you. Getting those opportunities will surely not come overnight, but consistent hard work and execution on your behalf will eventually help you get in position to come across available opportunities. While you're working hard and being consistent, other people will likely recognize and see your work ethic. There are times when you'll be heavily watched by other people and you won't even realize it. Always have the mindset that others could be watching your every move and you must always display your best while working every single day. Continue to work hard and diligently so you may one day be rewarded for all your efforts. You have what it takes to claim greatness. Have the right attitude so opportunities will be attracted to you like a magnet.

Even if you're currently not employed with a business, company, or agency that displays business excellence, having the right attitude can land you the opportunity to join one. When you're out in public, you never know who you may bump into. There are chief executive officers and business owners who walk around in our communities every day just like everyone else. On an ordinary day, it's possible to be in the presence of a businessperson who owns or has a great deal of power at a big company. As a matter of fact, there are many powerful business people who actively go out to recruit individuals to work for and with them. When you display the right attitude amongst people in the public, especially people you may consider to be strangers, you can potentially open a door of opportunity that will be beneficial for your life. While you're out in the community doing good work and displaying the right attitude at all times, good business people may notice you and offer you a job right on the spot. This is possible and it happens to a lot of people every single day. Also, some people you meet may even refer you to great companies or businesses that could use someone of your character and work ethic. Great work ethic is something a lot of people don't possess. One major downfall of a resume is that it cannot give an accurate and physical description of a person's work ethic. There isn't an actual rating scale created by our society that determines a person's work ethic. Also, if a rating scale was ever created to measure work ethic, would it possibly be up to standard for accurately measuring work ethic since it would be created by the hands of mankind? Along with that in mind, could all of mankind even come together and agree on a scale that accurately measures work ethic? This would be highly unlikely. There's already so much controversy over hundreds and thousands of topics that currently exist in the world today. Every single day that you walk on this earth, you never know when and where opportunity may present itself so you must be prepared. People can be a blessing to you. People change lives every day.

Your attitude during particular situations in life will assist in deciding your fate. During the most important highlights of your life, your attitude can either make or break your success. You were always destined to succeed and accomplish great things in life, but you can fall short of living up to your true potential when your attitude isn't right. Your destiny relies on your actions. When was the last time you evaluated your overall attitude and approach to life? Is your current attitude up to part for positioning yourself to receive greatness? Your attitude can assist with conquering any obstacles that get into your way. Greatness will always and forever be well within your reach. Open your hands and reach out for greatness, which stares you right in the face every single day. Nothing is impossible when you have faith and believe. Choose to always believe that you were meant to obtain greatness, regardless of what other people may think or say. Having the right attitude at the right moment will take you a long way. The right attitude will always lead you down a path for limitless blessings and opportunities.

FALL IN LOVE WITH HARD WORK

Hard work can simply bring about change that's worth desiring. Positive change is always worth fighting for and claiming. When there are certain things in life that you want to accomplish or become a part of, falling in love with hard work is the best way to make those things come true. You can somewhat distinguish hard work as being a true best friend in your life. A true best friend will always want the best for you in life. Hard work will lookout for you by opening doors of opportunity. It will also be active in protecting and guarding you at times. Throughout your life, hard work can protect you from falling into relaxed comfort zones or settling. When you become too relaxed or settle for less, you end up missing the mark of making your goals become a reality. In order to achieve as much as you possibly can while you're living, you must choose to build a strong bond between yourself and hard work. When building a strong bond with hard work, nothing is impossible and no dreams are too big for you to accomplish. Rather than falling in love with materialistic things or people that don't give back necessary assistance to help promote self-growth and empowerment, choose to fall in love with hard work. Fall in love with something that requires effort on your behalf, but in return pours back into you. Hard work helps mold you into becoming a phenomenal human being and a master at whatever craft you work on regularly. As we all know, it takes a certain amount of pressure to make a diamond. Being put under pressure in life isn't always a bad thing. From time to time, hard work will apply some type of pressure and uncomfortableness to come over you. During those particular moments in life, you have the option to embrace the pressure and see what you're capable of accomplishing. Let hard work become your best friend and accept the fact that pressure has the ability to push you to greatness. Hold hands with hard work and never let go.

If you truly want to encounter some of the most awesome experiences that life has to offer, it's not going to happen by just wishing and hoping. To experience the best that life has to offer, you definitely have to get busy putting in work on a consistent basis. Prayer is very important for seeking assistance from God, but you also have to do your part from a physical aspect. Every single day that you get the opportunity and privilege to live life, get the most out of it. When you wake up to begin your day, one of the first things that should cross your mind should be the opportunities available for you to experience that day. Each day is jam packed with many directions to go in and so many possible things to do. Through the eyes of a young child, life is like walking into a candy store with so many great sweets and deserts to choose from. In order to purchase those wonderful sweets and deserts, you must have money in your possession. With no money in your possession, you cannot get what you want. In life, if you don't get busy putting in work, you'll never come close to even scratching the surface of accomplishing and experiencing the great things that life has to offer. Time is ticking and you have absolutely no time to waste. Get busy now to shift the momentum of capturing greatness onto your side. If you've already taken the step to grind on a daily basis and get busy working, you've already placed yourself in position to reap great benefits. Get busy working now because your potential to elevate and become phenomenal depends on it.

Laziness isn't acceptable and doesn't have the privilege to stand in the same room with anything that represents greatness. Laziness is a stronghold that hinders an individual from making their dreams become a reality. Falling in love with hard work is your best way out to achieve your goals and dreams. Laziness is one of the reasons why there are so many people who cannot tap into their inner giant that silently lives on the inside of them. In order to tap into your talents, abilities, and hidden strengths, you must embrace hard work as a normal part of life. In our growing society today, choosing to settle for less and not having the drive to work has become a way of life for many people. This negative trend and way of life is continuously being passed down by people who have the wrong mindset about life. This is a trend that we all must work on together to destroy. For the sake of our younger generation of children, we must teach them that laziness will get you nowhere in life. It has also been taken into belief that many people perceive hard work as something they're allergic to. They view hard work as something that may do them harm rather than benefit them in the long run. This type of thinking is completely ridiculous. Let's reframe from this way of thinking and strive to be the phenomenal creatures that we all were destined to be. Hard work always pays off in the long run. Go hard every single day and watch your life change over time.

Another reason why many people in America choose to not work is because of the poorly managed distribution of government assistance throughout the country. There are so many American citizens today who receive government assistance and are more than capable of surviving without it. Thousands of Americans are taking advantage of government assistance with no hesitation on their part at all. On the other hand, there are American citizens who really need and deserve government assistance to make life a little easier for them. Examples of people who truly need government assistance are individuals who diligently look for employment so they can take care of their family, people who are unable to work due to disability, citizens who struggle to afford food because their household income is below the poverty level, and needy families who may have suffered a tremendous setback in life and need temporary assistance to get back on their feet. These are real examples of people who really need help and assistance, opposite from the fraudulent and lazy people in our society who are raping the system. If the distribution of government assistance was better handled in America, the fraudulent citizens that currently receive assistance would be forced to step up and work to take care of themselves. If they would choose to not step up, they would just wither away in the wind. If you're able to work and care for yourself, you should do it with great pride. Those who are able to work but choose to be lazy are taking up precious space on this earth.

In a way, some recipients of government assistance have fallen into the trap of becoming comfortable with receiving funds regularly rather than only using it as a temporary means of support until it's no longer needed. A large portion of the African American community has fallen into this deadly trap. It's possible that this trap could have been intentionally designed as a tactic to control different groups of people in America. When you have so many people depending on a particular resource for assistance, the operator that's controlling that resource has a great deal of power. People that possess a lot of power have control over many of the operations that take place in the world. At times, we all may encounter a setback in life or need assistance from others to get back on our feet. Experiencing these types of things is a natural part of life. One thing we all should never do is become comfortable with depending and relying on others for assistance permanently for the rest of our lives. If you're a person that's receiving government assistance and only need it temporarily, choose to make sure that the assistance you currently receive remains temporary and doesn't become a permanent part of your life. You're strong and wise enough to survive in this world. You may encounter some setbacks and shortcomings, but you have the power to bounce back and be victorious. Never be ashamed to be in need of assistance or help. It happens to the best of us. One thing a person should be ashamed of is choosing to be comfortable with forever relying on assistance from others when they're able to stand strong without it. If this is you, change your mindset and work hard to survive. Work hard and become an example of what it takes to be phenomenal.

Hard work has a great way of producing positive results when you do everything the right way. Part of doing everything the right way is linked to the element of consistency. For you math lovers in the world, achieving positive results is accomplished by a simple mathematical equation of addition. Hard work plus consistency equals positive results. The hard work you produce must be combined with a flow of consistency to get the end results you actually want. A slight break or disturbance in your consistency will have an impact on how long it could take you to reach a goal that you're trying to accomplish. Anything that can disrupt your flow should be avoided if possible. Your time is sensitive and you should be careful when you decide to take time off from your goals and dreams. In reality, if you decide to take a few days or a week off from working hard to accomplish a goal or task, that may potentially set you back several months from completing whatever you're trying to accomplish. Taking too much time off continues to stretch that gap between you and success. At times, we all need to take a short break to relax and build up our energy to move forward, but your breaks should be limited and not used at unnecessary moments. Consistency is a huge piece of the puzzle that you need to get where you want to go. When you're consistent in your work, momentum will be on your side. You control the outcome of many situations with your actions and efforts. For everything that you work hard to achieve, always choose to do it with great consistency. When you're consistent on the regular basis, there's only a matter of time before you're met face to face with achieving whatever goal you're chasing. Hard work combined with regular consistency won't fail you.

When you're physically working hard on things that you want to create or accomplish, you're bound to successfully meet the finish line and claim victory in the race you're running. Nothing in this world comes easy and requires no effort. If everything in life could be easily obtained with no effort at all, there would be no such thing as hard work. The existence of hard work in our lives really makes us all better people. As a positive benefit, hard work actually has the ability to instill appreciation into people. When you work hard for something and finally achieve it, you quickly develop a high level of respect and admiration for everything you've done leading up to the point of reaching your goal. Those long days, long nights, constant sacrifices, constant struggles, and consistent hard work means a lot to you. These are things that you'll remember forever. That's a lot to cherish by any person. With everything you've done to accomplish certain tasks, goals, or dreams, you never want your hard work to go unrecognized and unappreciated. Who in their right mind would want their hard work to be easily forgotten? If it wasn't for your efforts of hard work in everything you do, you wouldn't be standing and walking in greatness. You wouldn't be the strong and phenomenal person you are today if it wasn't for all the hard work that you've put in leading up to this point. Continue to allow hard work to transform your life and open doors of opportunity. Those who work hard will receive amazing blessings in return. Enjoy life and live for the grind of hard work.

If you're not in love with hard work at this very moment, you have the ability to change that right now. There's no better time to make a positive change in your life than now. Why wait until tomorrow or the following day to fall in love with hard work? Tomorrow is never promised and we should never put things off later that we can simply do today. If you're a person who's totally against hard work, you must change your mindset of how you view hard work and what it can do for your life. Hard work can take you certain places in life that are considered well above mediocre or average platforms. If you want to soar gracefully above the clouds like eagles, you have to put in hard work. As long as you choose to keep pressing forward and work to get pass challenges, you have the ability to overcome anything that stands in your way. Greatness can be achieved by putting forth hard work on a consistent basis. Hard work will definitely separate you from other people who don't have your type of mentality. Your strong work ethic and determination won't allow you to sit at the same table with slackers. You wouldn't fit in with slackers, so your heart and mind would lead you into another direction. Hard work will draw you closer to people who are more like you, which is very beneficial to your growth. You always need a good circle of individuals around you. We all need to practice continuous growth throughout our walk of life. As we all learn and grow, we become better people over time. If you're already in love with hard work, continue to let that fire burn and never let it perish. Share and tell other people about your love for hard work. Other people will truly listen and take in your experience of putting in hard work. With your words, you may encourage someone else to fall in love with hard work as well. This world needs more brave people to encourage others to fall in love with hard work. Encourage your close friends, family members, and even co-workers to work hard in everything they do. Along with encouraging others, continue to let hard work be one of your main tools to reach success. With your strong work ethic, you can go anywhere. The sky is the limit.

KEEP YOUR EYES ON THE PRIZE

There are so many beautiful and astonishing things that life has to offer to every breathing human being. Life presents opportunities for all of us to do great things such as bringing creative ideas into existence that benefit the world, accomplishing goals, helping others, and mastering certain crafts. If there's anything in particular that you desperately want to have or do, keep your eyes on that prize and go all in until you have claimed it. Along the way of making your dreams become a reality, you'll be tested with challenges or obstacles that will cause the view between you and your grand prize to become a little blurry. When you're chasing success, this comes along with the territory. Regardless of any challenges or obstacles that present themselves in the midst of your grind, choose to remain focused on claiming your prize. You were created with the strength to keep pressing forward even when things get a little tough within your journey to pursue goals. Always keep your eyes laser focused on being victorious and claiming greatness. Failure shouldn't be on your brain when you're thinking about how to claim your prize. Pull out a pen and strategize a plan of execution. Be creative and find ways to overcome obstacles that present themselves when you're trying to win. You're a winner, so think like one. Do things that winners are known to do. Choose to walk with great confidence and have unmeasurable faith like real winners do. Choose to bounce back from setbacks when you're slightly bumped off course like real winners do. At the end of the day, it's all on you to claim your prize of victory. Keep your eyes on the prize and enjoy the experience of victory.

There are several strategies that you can use to stay focused when unfavorable circumstances create a blur between you and the prize you so greatly desire. When challenges come about, you must be able to counteract the elements of the situation to continue moving forward. One strategy that can be used to help you focus more on claiming prizes during difficult situations is making the reason behind wanting the prize to be about other people and not yourself. In most cases, when we're striving to claim a prize, we're mainly going after the prize for our own personal benefit. How many times have you strived to obtain or win something for the sake of others? When have you ever chosen to put others before yourself? Doing things in the honor of others is something that most people never take into consideration when living life. Everything that we do shouldn't always be just about ourselves. Doing something in the honor of others is a true action of unselfishness. Being unselfish is a great characteristic to possess. When you're unselfish in your ways, you have the ability to show unconditional love and respect toward others. The world needs more unselfish people in it. Too many people walk around every single day only concerned with what they can do to benefit themselves. There's absolutely nothing wrong with going hard and breaking your back to get what you want out of life, but your desire to do things for others shouldn't be an empty bucket.

Think about your family and friends that play a very active role in your life. When you're on the move, aggressively chasing your dreams and goals, take some of those situations and place the important people in your life behind the driver seat of your reason for doing what you do. When you do certain things for the sake of people who mean a lot to you, you'll have the tendency to go harder and not give up until you've accomplished your goal. When you feel like other people are counting on you and everything you're doing will definitely help them out, your drive to keep going forward becomes like a freight train that's pushing ahead with great power. If the goal ahead is becoming a little blurry because of challenges or difficulty, place your reason for chasing your goal onto the head of those who are close to you. The space between you and your prize that may have seemed to be a little blurry may start to clear up a bit. You'll be more focused on the end result rather than the challenges at hand. The challenges and obstacles that present themselves may cause a distraction for a brief moment when they arrive, but you have the ability to get back focused on the task at hand. Fight the good fight of keeping your eyes on the prize.

On some occasions, you should allow another human being to be the primary reason for your desire to take on a task or chase a goal. There's absolutely nothing wrong with going after something for the sake of others and leaving your wants or personal desires on the sideline for later. People make sacrifices for other people every single day. Some parents make daily sacrifices for their children and are proud of it. There have been special people who have lived and died in the act of honoring those who they deeply care about. We have great historic leaders such as Dr. Martin Luther King Jr. who strived for the civil rights and justice of all African Americans. He also strived for peace and equality for all mankind. Dr. King dedicated his life toward trying to persuade all human beings to love one another regardless of race, gender, nationality, creed, or skin color. Dr. King died in the process of doing his best to help make the world a better place. Take the focus off of yourself sometimes and place it on other people. Other people can give you strength to keep your eyes on the prize. Fight for your prize and continue to stay laser focused on it until it's yours. If you can truly believe that it's yours, there's absolutely nothing that can stop you from becoming victorious. The people you deeply care about and love may be depending on you to claim a prize for them. Don't let them down and don't let yourself down.

One very important action that's needed to claim your prize and achieve success is talking your victory into existence. To get your prize, you must announce to the universe that you're declaring victory by any means. Declaring victory by any means refers to the necessary actions you're willing to take without any let up. This takes great confidence and bravery for a person to do. If you're willing to step out on a limb and claim victory, even when it has yet to arrive, you'll give yourself a good initial start. The way you begin a journey sets the tone for everything else that follows. Why not use your tongue to set the tone? Words are very powerful, especially when you speak them into existence. The power of the tongue shouldn't be taken for granted or taken lightly. The words that come out of your mouth have the ability to change lives and situations forever. This is why it's extremely important to be careful with the words you choose to speak into existence. When chasing your prize, you never want to speak words of negativity over your capabilities. If you preach words that don't express your ability to reach victory, you've already lost the battle of getting into the zone of winning. You must speak words of victory when you're talking about your life. Speaking words of victory places you in a zone to focus and lock in on your prize. When you're chasing your prizes in life, you must talk as if you're truly destined to obtain the deep desires of your heart. If you stay true to using words that declare victory in the things you do, there's nothing in this world that can stop you. When other people in the world speak over your life, their words don't hold has much power as what you choose to say about yourself. Stay true to declaring victory in your life and that prize you want will soon be in your possession. Everything is on you. Choose to believe because you're nothing short of phenomenal.

The energy that you're using during your daily grind is placed in specific areas of your life. The way we spend our time every single day is as equally important as what we decide to do with our energy. Within one single day, you only have so much energy to use. Once that energy is all used, you have to reboot yourself to tackle the next day in front of you. With that being said, a great portion of the energy we use on the daily basis should be put toward chasing a prize. You don't have time or energy to waste at all. The time and date at which you'll be leaving this earth is completely unknown to you. If you really think you know when your time on this earth will be up, it's highly suggested that you rethink that idea. This is why you should always put a huge portion of the energy you possess toward going after lifelong prizes. It's understandable that you must put a good portion of your energy toward required responsibilities. Your required responsibilities may consist of things such as going to work, taking care of your children and family, exercising to maintain good health, fulfilling your religious duties, focusing on your education, and even more. Even with all of the required responsibilities you have on your plate, you must make time to put energy toward your prize. In all, some of the required responsibilities that were just mentioned may possibly be a prize that you're striving to achieve. You may be striving to go back to school to earn a degree or certification. Also, you may have started exercising on the regular basis to get into good physical shape. Whatever prize you have your eyes set on, it needs a great portion of your time and energy in order for you to claim it.

Make a bold and important decision to place a great portion of your energy into your dreams and goals. When you're up and about throughout the day, your energy flows into the direction of where your attention goes. Many people make the simple mistake of using most of their energy to do things that don't add value to their lives or make them better people. Would you be so eager to allow precious energy to go to waste? Your attention should be locked into certain things that will allow you to grow and achieve success. Some of the people we come across in our daily lives can surely rob us of our attention and focus. Some people who may envy or dislike you will choose to make throwing you off of your game as one of their top priorities every day. These particular people can also be categorized as your haters. Your haters never want to see you shine bright like a diamond. They really get pleasure out of seeing you during your times of struggle or misfortune. Some of your haters wake up every single day on a mission to make your life miserable if they can or if you allow them to do so. In most cases, your haters may be jealous of you because of the success or accomplishments you've achieved. Pay these types of people no attention at all because they want to see you fail in everything you do. You've been created to succeed and overcome any obstacle that presents itself in your life. How much do you value the life you've been blessed with? Placing a significant amount of your energy toward chasing your prize shows the dedication and hunger you have for being great. Many people will be able to see your determination for chasing your dreams and greatly admire it. Your dream and prize chasing could potentially create a spark that will ignite someone else to get busy living. Transferring encouragement and hope to others can make the world a better place. Putting an enormous amount of energy into chasing your prize will surely make your own personal world a better place. Run your race and smile while doing so. You have plenty of reasons to smile because greatness, achievements, and success are laid out for you to claim.

KEEP PRESSING FORWARD

Within this journey called life, there are moments where life can throw you curve balls of challenges and difficulties. Those challenges and difficulties may press down hard on you like heavy weights. Living a life where challenges, difficulties, and setbacks don't cross your path is completely impossible. When these situations present themselves, it's in your best interest and beneficial for your entire future to keep pressing forward. Even when it seems that pressing forward will be tough to bare, make the decision to continue to press forward anyway. Later on in the future, you'll be pleased that you didn't back down while under pressure. Continuing to fight while under pressure creates personal growth. Also, once you're beyond one hurdle in life, never be naive and think that no more hurdles will occur in your life. Pressing forward through your current challenges and difficulties will make you stronger for other battles in the near future. One of the best teachers in life is experience. The experience you gain within your difficulties right now will allow you to use the tools you've acquired for future battles. Use those tools for your personal benefit. Keep those tools in your toolbox, which is your mind. Your mind is one of the biggest storage facilities in the entire world. When the time comes for you to put your tools to work, pull them out of your toolbox with no hesitation. No matter how big the hurdle is, keep pressing forward. Give yourself a chance to grow and walk into greatness.

Beyond your current troubles are brighter days. It may be kind of difficult to see brighter days ahead when dark clouds are currently raining down on your head. Fog and mist restricts your view of what's ahead of you. Sometimes when we're experiencing hardships, our mind can get fogged up with negativity and pain that prohibits accurate decision making on our part. Making bad decisions is where we begin to create more trouble for ourselves. When you have one problem or issue going on, you never want to start adding more problems and create an even heavier load. The best thing to do when the storms of life are raining down on your head is to try your best to remain calm. In an effort to remain calm, think about how your current state is only visiting you temporarily. After a temporary problem has run its course, it has no choice but to exit your life. From that point, you continue on living. Beyond temporary troubles are brighter and happier days. Using this way of thinking may not necessarily make the dark clouds and rain go away, but it gives you hope and will decrease the fog you're currently experiencing in your storm. Having hope will always help you through your storms in life. There are many great things to look forward to in your life beyond temporary problems. Your future is filled with more accomplishments and success for you to obtain. Your life is like a book. It consists of many pages and chapters. One particular problem in your life can be just a couple of pages in one chapter. On a much smaller scale, a particular problem that you're facing could be just one page or a paragraph. Every challenge or difficulty is different, which means that the time frames will be different as well. At times, many of us have made the mistake of making a problem or difficulty bigger than it actually should be in our lives. Dragging out problems beyond their expiration date wastes precious time and energy that could be used for much greater things. During times of difficulties, always believe that you have more positive days awaiting you. Keep your faith and stay strong.

During a difficult and temporary situation that occurs in your life, another thing you should strongly take into consideration is that the pain you're experiencing within your difficulty may be a blessing in disguise. Blessings come in many different forms. Often times, we may not always recognize a blessing at the beginning of its course. It's possible that pain can sometimes come into your life as an instrument to mold you into a better person. Take a minute and think about how a precious diamond is made. It takes an enormous amount of pressure to accurately make a diamond. In comparison to the pressure that's needed to make a diamond, sometimes it takes a tone of pressure to mold a human being into becoming their absolute best. Experiencing pain and pressure can be a bit uncomfortable for us, but it may be necessary for personal growth. In order for you to reach your highest potential, you may have to go through a little unwanted pain. You may have to encounter some bumps, bruises, and setbacks. A setback can sometimes allow you to refocus and restructure a plan that you've created. You may get knocked down, but you have the ability to get back up and keep pressing forward. You were born to be a conqueror that can stand strong in the face of adversity. Accept that temporary pain can be an unusual beginning for achieving something great in the long run. Every single road to victory isn't pretty.

During certain moments in life, you just have to smile at your troubles and difficulties, knowing that victory and success is right down the road. This may sound like a strange thing to do for some people, but every day you should continue to smile. It's better to just smile rather than always wearing a frown because your difficulties will be present whether you like it or not. You have to get out of your feelings and get into an atmosphere of faith. Are you going to allow difficulties to keep you from smiling and enjoying life? It's definitely not worth it. Continue to smile regardless of how long temporary difficulties may last. In some cases, the temporary difficulties in our lives may have an expiration date that's much farther off than we think. As human beings, sometimes we choose to put a lot of trust and confidence into certain predictions we make. If our predictions don't come out as planned, there's a possibility that the outcome will leave us feeling like complete failures. When things don't go our way, sometimes we may feel like the walls of life have caved in on us. We must save ourselves from experiencing this type of self-inflicting pain. Our predictions of how certain things should operate or transpire don't always correspond with the reality of life. For our own good, it may be best to never heavily lean on our own understanding of a situation, but accept that things will work themselves out in the way they were intended. This is part of having faith and choosing to stay in good character. Faith can act as a blanket of comfort that gives you peace. Even when storms and chaos is all around us, we have the ability to still be calm and collective. Doing this helps us to concentrate on taking care of business and focusing our attention on being happy. Crack a smile every day and make the decision to live in peace.

During his amazing career as a professional basketball player, Michael Jordan gave the world a short glimpse of how to keep pressing forward when faced with a temporary problem. If you don't know or have never heard of Michael Jordan, there's no way that you live on the planet earth. Michael Jordan is arguably one of the greatest basketball players to ever play the game. During his tenure in the national basketball association, he dominated the league and did it in a fashion that had never been seen before. When Michael entered the NBA, the game of basketball changed forever. Back in 1997, game five of the NBA Finals was a game that most die-hard basketball fans will remember forever. Leading up to game five of the NBA Finals, Michael had developed flu like symptoms. Having the flu is very serious and can be life threatening if not treated properly. Despite having the flu, Michael took it upon himself to still suit up for game five of the NBA finals. He figured that his teammates needed him to play in game five for them to have a chance at capturing the championship trophy. Another dominant force in the NBA stood in their way of becoming champions. In this particular championship series, the Chicago Bulls were facing the Utah Jazz, a dominant western conference team that had a championship pedigree. The Jazz were hungry for a championship and they were willing to put up a great fight. During this particular time in the NBA, both the Bulls and Jazz were by far the best two teams in the league. There were future hall of fame players on both sides of the basketball. If Michael didn't suit up for game five, you could probably say that it was all over for the Bulls. The absence of Michael in game five would have completely changed the entire series.

As Michael walked to the locker room and proceeded to take the court for game five, you could see nothing short of uncomfortableness in his face. The flu had really taken a toll on him and he was doing his very best to deal with it. Some of Michael's teammates were worried about him playing in this game with the flu. Also, the Bulls were playing game five in unfriendly territory. They were on the road in Utah. Road games can be the toughest games to win in professional sports. The Bulls had to deal with battling the Jazz players on their court and a loud roaring crowd of Jazz fans. Even though Michael was going through the motions of dealing with the flu, his mind and focus was in the right place. Winning game five was on his radar. As the game tipped off, Michael went to work. During the first quarter, he started off a bit slow as far as scoring points. At one point, the Bulls were down by double digit points in the first quarter and there was confusion on the face of Michael. However, Michael began to take things up a notch in the second quarter. By halftime, he had scored a total of twenty-one points. Michael was carrying the load of the team even with his condition. While taking a rest on the sidelines, Michael could be seen slumped over in his seat for the most part. His teammates and other staff members were attending to him as he sat on the sidelines. Despite dealing with the flu, Michael went on to score a total of thirty-eight points and led his team to victory over the Jazz. At the end of the game, you could see his teammate Scottie Pippen helping him off of the court. Michael had given every ounce of energy that he had. Michael demonstrated a great example of the human will to keep pressing forward during uncomfortable circumstances.

Just as Michael showed the human will to keep pressing forward, every single person on this earth has the ability to do the same. When times get hard and rough, when grey clouds rain on your parade, and when everything seems to be up against you, you still have the strength to keep pressing forward. No matter what circumstances come across your path, you must continue to keep pressing forward at all times. What would have happened if Michael had given up and quit during game five of the NBA Finals? If he had given up, the Jazz would have most likely captured the NBA title that year. Michael continued to keep pressing forward and led his team to be crowned as the NBA champions. What would happen if you give up and quit on what you want to accomplish in life? If you quit and give up during unfavorable circumstances, you'll never be able to capture victory that's well within your reach. You have what it takes to keep pressing forward, so step out on faith and keep pushing. Give every ounce of energy that you have left in your body to be crowned victorious. If you're totally drained and have to crawl your way to the finish line, then do it. As long as you don't give up on yourself in the heat of the battle, you'll ultimately succeed. Things may get ugly, but just know that most victories are won in situations that aren't so pretty or glamorous. Some situations can be a dog fight, but you have what it takes to be victorious.

During this journey called life, challenges and difficulties will mostly come about at unexpected moments. These unexpected surprises are the type of shocking events we label as unwelcomed. For the most part, we all hope and pray that the frequent surprises that come into our lives are more toward our personal liking. However, we don't have the power to selectively choose every single event that will take place in our lives. Therefore, it's a very strong possibility that monkey wrenches will fall into some of our plans and disrupt our entire flow. Well-designed plans to achieve success are subject to be thrown off course when challenges and difficulties arrive. Have you ever had a well-designed plan of execution to obtain a specific goal and all of a sudden disaster strikes? This can be a very heavy blow to take depending on certain circumstances. At times, disaster has the ability to strike a blow so heavy that it makes us want to give up on everything. Regardless of the severity of certain blows you encounter in life, you should never give up on anything. Your life holds significant value and is well worth cherishing. You must never give up on all the hard work you've put in toward accomplishing your dreams. Your work ethic and accomplishments are way too valuable to be easily left on the side of the road. It's important for you to know and honestly believe that you were born to be great. Monkey wrenches that are thrown into our well-designed plans may slow us down temporarily, but we all possess great strength to keep pressing forward. When you encounter a setback or challenge, instead of choosing to give up on life or give up on accomplishing a goal, choose to keep pressing forward. Press forward through all the pain, heartache, and disappointments. Continue to keep pressing forward with great confidence and watch your life transform. As long as you continue to keep pressing forward, you're bound to reach the light at the end of the tunnel. At the end of every tunnel is victory for you to claim.

THE COMPANY YOU KEEP

The people that we spend a great amount of time with and are very close to us have a major impact on our entire lives. These people include close friends, family members, and significant others. Depending on what these individuals bring to the table, they have the ability to make a positive or negative impact on our lives. This is why it's extremely important to be cautious of who you allow to become an active participant in your everyday life. The company you keep can act as an important element in the achievements you obtain or the failures and heartache you encounter. Your company may also have a heavy influence on the decisions you make on the regular basis. Everyone doesn't give the best advice when pertaining to certain situations. In our society, there are many people who go around giving other people advice about how to handle certain situations when they in fact lack true understanding and success in those areas themselves. It's highly likely that there's a person with this type of characteristic among the people you know personally. There's no way that a person who's struggling in a certain area in their lives can give you good advice on that same particular topic. How can you validate a person's opinion on a particular subject matter that they lack experience or more importantly success? For the most part, there's a slim to none possibility to validate a person's opinion in this case. The company you keep should consist of people who truly care about you and won't cause you harm. If necessary, you may have to distance yourself from certain people who are currently close to you in order to receive blessings and enjoy life to the fullest. Be wise in choosing the company you keep. No one is exempt from being removed from your circle if they can't be a blessing to you.

There are simply two different categories that the people you consider to be your friends will fall under. These two categories are the pretenders and true friends. The pretenders in your life are merely disguising themselves in a phony image that looks as if they really care about you and wish the best for you. Underneath those false disguises is the true nature of individuals who are not your real friends. A pretender may choose to be close to you in an effort to possibly sabotage or disrupt anything good that comes your way. Pretenders may also choose to be close to you in an effort to take advantage of good resources you own. In all, the motive of a pretender is never positive. This type of behavior is labeled as unethical in our society. In addition, the practice of ethical behavior is currently at an all-time low. Are you able to recognize pretenders that may be currently disguising themselves as your true friends? Pretenders are people that we all must work on avoiding. If pretenders stick around in our lives too long, they may become successful in executing their overall motive. Try your best to avoid pretenders at all costs. Even while pretenders are wearing their disguises, their true nature and motive may tend to leak out and be noticeable. Pretenders are human and they can possibly make a mistake by unintentionally letting out a small piece of their true character. If you witness something like this among the people you strongly consider as your friends, it may be wise to start giving your relationship with these individuals a little more thought. It seems that being a pretender is quite a hard job. It's sad that some people put so much time and effort into portraying a false image of themselves. All of that extra time and effort could be put toward loving and caring for other people. Beware of the pretenders that try to get comfortable in your life. They're dead weight that must be left behind.

The true friends in your life are the people who really have your back and your best interest at heart. These individuals should get the majority of your time when you're spending time with other people. There are many great benefits that come along with having real true friends in your life. True friends love and care for you unconditionally. At moments when you're feeling down and defeated, true friends will be there to motivate you and lift you back up. Regardless of how strong or tough you may be, you're susceptible to encountering difficult situations where help from other people is needed. Even the greatest leaders and most self-driven individuals need help from time to time. True friends will also give you honest and helpful advice. Being honest is considered ethical behavior that our society strongly encourages. Honesty is one of the most powerful elements within relationships. True friends will give you an honest response when a question is asked, even if they feel you may disagree with their response. True friends care about you enough to share their true feelings with you. When someone really cares about you, they'll never intentionally give you advice that will damage you or lead you to committing actions that are harmful to your life. When you've been blessed with true friends, make sure you treat them right to keep them around long-term. True friends won't disappoint you, so don't make the mistake of disappointing them. A true friend is precious cargo that needs to travel with you during this journey called life.

If you haven't taken time to evaluate and review the type of company you surround yourself with, now is the perfect time to do so. Continuing to put this off at a later time will eventually cause more damage to your life if pretenders are within your circle. It's very important that you start cleaning house and taking action right now for the sake of your future. As you begin this process, make sure you don't leave out any of the people you spend a lot of time with and those you consider to be very close to you. Include all of your close friends, family members, and even co-workers if possible. If you're in a relationship with someone, married, or dating certain individuals, these people should also be included in your evaluation and review. In your spare time, take a sheet of paper and write down the names of each and every person that's close to you. The length of your list may be short or long. At the most, you'll only have to use one sheet of paper. Even if you have a very big family and a good number of friends, all of these individuals won't make your list. For the most part, many family members are only seen during reunions or family gatherings. Also, we don't see some of our friends that often and usually talk to them by telephone occasionally. When creating your list for evaluation and review, make sure you only include the people you have consistent contact with and talk to at least weekly. Once you've created your list, take a good amount of time with each name and think about the type of impact they have on your life. Furthermore, think deeply and label each person on the list as either a pretender or a true friend.

After evaluating how each and every person on your list affects your overall life, you should then be able to decide whose worthy of being close to you and who needs to be cut from your circle. During your evaluation and assessing your relationship with each person on the list, you must have an open mind and be completely honest with yourself about what each person brings to the relationship. At many times, we don't like to be honest with ourselves. This is classified as a common human error. Facing the truth and being honest with ourselves can sometimes be a scary situation for many of us. We often reframe from being honest with ourselves by creating an image in our mind that reflects what we want our lives to look like. Choosing to not see certain things for what they truly are can cause significant harm to us. Facing the truth can sometimes hurt, but facing the truth is also a good practice of maturity. After assessing your relationship with the people on your list, the people who don't have a positive influence on your life must be given the boot. Ending certain relationships with people can be tough and a hard pill to swallow, but it must be done when necessary. Making the proper adjustments to save your life is a necessity. As you begin to give the pretenders in your life the boot, you'll begin to drastically witness positive change. Doors of opportunity may begin to open up that were not present in the past. When you have the wrong people around you, many good opportunities and blessings will be missed. Pretenders in your life can be like a blindfold over your eyes that prevent you from seeing positive light. For the sake of having a great future, embrace your true friends and dismiss all of the pretenders.

Reevaluating the culture that exists within your circle on occasions may be a good idea to put into action. Just like when a person takes time every so often to do a clean sweep of their home and search for unnecessary belongings that need to be thrown away, you should make an effort to reevaluate your circle every so often to see if any true friends have turned into pretenders. In life, people change all the time and there's a good chance that some people you consider as friends today may turn into pretenders later on down the road. If true friends switch up on you and become pretenders, they have to be given the boot. Treat your circle just like you treat your home. If you're a home owner that likes to keep your home as clean as possible, you may conduct a clean sweep of your home at least three times a year on average. Especially when the weather and seasons begin to change, most people begin to conduct their clean sweeps. During a clean sweep, you may throw away old clothes, shoes, furniture, kid toys, and other objects that are no longer being used in your house. Opposite from the general cleaning you conduct on a weekly basis, conducting a clean sweep can sometimes be a bit more tedious because you're basically searching every inch of the house. It's very beneficial to conduct a clean sweep as often as you can because it will keep down the volume of unnecessary junk in your home. On certain occasions, conduct a clean sweep within your circle of friends. If you don't find any unnecessary dead weight that's holding you down or causing any negativity, that's a major plus for you. If you do find negative people and friends who aren't helping you grow as a person, you need to start taking out the trash that's stinking up your circle. Your circle of influence is a very important part of your life that should be kept in good condition. Maintain the stability of love, encouragement, support, and positivity within your circle.

The company you keep has an enormous impact on your entire life. Having the wrong crowd around you will destroy or interfere with your chances of being great and obtaining special blessings. Make sure the company you keep is free of pretenders and back stabbers. Having the right circle of people in your life is certainly a matter of life and death. True friends bring about positive rays of sunshine into our lives that makes us feel loved. Pretenders can cause heartache, pain, and trouble that could possibly lead you down a path of destruction. There are so many people who lived on this earth at one point in time and lost their lives at the hands of a pretender. Behind the many holding cells within correctional facilities all over the world, you can find murders, rapists, thieves, and woman beaters who may have once disguised themselves as true friends to people before committing their crimes. An enormous number of people that are walking the streets of civilization have committed many heinous crimes against citizens and haven't been caught for their actions. This should make you be highly cautious of who you allow to be heavily involved in your everyday life. Don't let pretenders keep you from living a life that's drama free. Continue to build meaningful relationships with true friends that help you grow and motivate you to be the best that you can possibly be. Since you're a phenomenal individual, the company you keep should be phenomenal as well. Any group you're affiliated with should consist of people who share interests and morals about life that are similar to yours. Keep true friends in your circle that will assist you with achieving and conquering anything. Your ability to obtain greatness depends on it. As you continue your journey through life, never lose focus of keeping the right people in your circle.

APPETITE FOR SUCCESS

In order for any person on this earth to capture their dreams and achieve success, one must have a strong inner desire and appetite for success. When you have a true hunger for something you desperately want to claim as your own, you'll likely have the mentality to do whatever it takes to capture the desires of your heart. If there's an inner burning desire inside of you to accomplish something in life, your actions to hunt down that goal will jump into high gear if you're a true warrior within the battle grounds of life. If you currently don't have an appetite for success, it's not too late to develop one. Today is the perfect day to start developing an appetite for success. Are there any phenomenal goals or dreams you wish to obtain in your lifetime? Search deep down inside your soul and find at least one particular thing that you really want out of life. For many adults, there may have been certain things you desperately dreamed about accomplishing as a child. Children use their imagination very well and have a unique way of developing a hunger for specific things. The hunger for wanting to do something great in life is heavily intertwined with the desires of the heart. If necessary, have a deep conversation with yourself to find out what you truly want out of life. Once you've discovered that special thing or phenomenal goal you want to accomplish, begin to push and encourage yourself to develop a strong appetite to handle your business. Only the strong and tenacious pursuers of success will rightfully capture their goals. When you have an appetite for success, it's only a matter of time before you're victorious. Continue to be hungry for success and run toward the opportunities that life presents to you.

There are many people in this world that display a great example of having an appetite for success. These particular people have a strong motor of putting forth an enormous amount of effort to achieve success. When you think about certain people like this, former NBA great Kobe Bryant may be one of those individuals that come to mind. Kobe is recognized by many current NBA players, former NBA players, and basketball fans as one of the greatest basketball players of all time. At the prime of his career, Kobe displayed talents and skills that allowed him to dominate the league. Whenever Kobe walked onto the basketball court, he had this tenacious attitude that was very different from many other players. He would carry himself in such a way that put fear into the heart of his opponents. While winning multiple NBA championships throughout his career, Kobe's appetite for success was shown through his unbelievable work ethic. Kobe would spend countless hours in the gym toward perfecting his craft. At many times, Kobe would be seen as the first person to make it to team practices and the last person to leave. Kobe, aka "Black Mamba", had a unique way of perfecting his craft through what he called the "Mamba Mentality". Using the mamba mentality consists of being on a constant pursuit to be the best version of yourself. This mindset can be associated with continuous growth. On a constant basis, Kobe did everything in his power to be the best basketball player he could possibly be. Through all of the countless hours of practice and hard work he put in, Kobe was able to claim much success during his entire career as a professional basketball player. Kobe won multiple championships, individual awards, and broke many records that were set by players before him. Use Kobe's mamba mentality to assist you with developing an appetite for success. Being on a constant pursuit to be the best version of yourself will give you positive results. You only get one life to live, so strive toward being the best version of yourself.

In order to prosper in today's world, you must definitely have an appetite for wanting to do something great and maximizing your potential for survival. Having a goal to accomplish something great gives you a sense of purpose about your life. It gives you another reason for wanting to live other than being around for your friends or love ones. Goal setting gives you another reason to smile when you first wake up in the morning. Another day on earth means another day of opportunity to do something great. Opportunity gives you the chance to continue striving for what you desperately want out of life. Having an appetite for maximizing your potential of survival will drive you toward doing research on survival tactics and developing certain behaviors that will allow you to stay on earth a bit longer. When most people want to know how they can add years onto their life, they do their homework and research. In our society today, the internet has been very beneficial for finding information. We can find information about healthy foods to eat, natural herbs to consume, and exercise practices that will help increase our potential for survival on earth. As far as developing certain behaviors that will allow us to live longer, we must force ourselves to routinely perform daily actions that will greatly benefit our lives. Developing behaviors such as being more aware of our surroundings, practicing ethical reasoning and decision making, having a well-balanced diet, exercising on the regular basis, and practicing good stress management are a few things we can do to help us have a better chance of living longer. Choose to have an appetite for maximizing your potential of survival while you're blessed to be living.

The world we live in today is a challenging place to survive. While maneuvering through this challenging world, you must be aware that the job market is very competitive, nutritional resources are limited, illnesses and diseases are ending lives at a rapid pace, and criminal activity is continuing to rise every single day. Some people have it harder than others in regards to survival on earth. The world we live in is like a jungle. In a jungle, one of the main objectives for wild animals is survival. You have to eat and prevent yourself from being eaten in the jungle. Wild animals also have to claim territory as their own. Claiming territory is not an easy task, neither is defending it from others. There's so much that goes on inside a wild jungle on a daily basis. In our society, having an appetite to succeed will help you combat the challenges of the world. In order to obtain or accomplish certain things in life, you'll have to compete against other people sometimes. Many animals in the wild have to compete amongst each other for survival. Only the courageous will be able to combat the challenges that life presents and come out on top. You were definitely born with the strength to be courageous. This world is tough and you must develop thick skin to sustain certain blows that will strike you. Hard striking blows from the world are liable to strike you at any given moment. This comes along with the territory of being on earth. When you have an appetite for success, you'll be able to hang with the best that occupy this jungle called earth. Have an appetite for success and continue to be phenomenal.

Having a true appetite for success will spark your interest to start grinding and working harder. Grinding and working hard is the only way you'll be able to witness your dreams transform into reality. At the beginning of every single morning when you wake up, you should be thankful for another day to live. Every morning that you're given the opportunity to see the sun rise, you need to pray and thank God for another beautiful day to experience life. Another day to live on this earth gives you the opportunity to make your dreams come true and help other people that may need your assistance. This is what makes every second of your life extremely valuable. Why not grind hard to accomplish goals and make other people lives better in the process? A great number of the actions you take in life will have an everlasting effect on other people. Grinding hard will open doors of opportunity for both you and others. At times, God may use you to be a blessing for someone else. For example, if you have unique skills or abilities that can get certain things accomplished, your skills or abilities may come in handy to help someone else who's struggling and is in dying need of assistance. A person with a good heart will sometimes go out of their way to help other people who would benefit from their assistance. At certain times, there's nothing wrong with putting in work to help others even when you're not going to personally benefit from the effort you're putting forth. Every so often, take time to be selfless and devote your attention to assist other people. Blessings do come to those who genuinely seek to help other people. If you have the strength to grind hard for your own benefit, you most certainly have enough energy left over to grind for others. Allow your appetite for success to send your desire to grind hard into overdrive. As long as you continue grinding, positive results are bound to follow. Continue to stay hungry for success and grind hard every single day like there's no tomorrow in your future. With this type of mindset, you'll definitely succeed.

Having a true appetite for success combined with consistent effort will make you unstoppable. Unstoppable individuals have the ability to do great things in life. When you accomplish a goal that you've been consistently working on for a great deal of time, you'll ultimately get an indescribable feeling that's somewhat mixed with joy and gratefulness. It feels good to reflect back on a long journey and see your growth. As long as we continue to practice self-growth, our lives will get better. Embrace basketball legend Kobe Bryant's mamba mentality and be amazed at what you accomplish over time. Are you curious about what you're capable of accomplishing when you strive to be your best? Throughout your life, make positive daily strides toward becoming the best version of yourself. You most definitely can't become the best version of yourself overnight, which means you'll have to put in much effort over a period of time. Making consistent effort to become the best version of yourself can motivate other people to do the same. For many human beings, seeing someone demonstrating a behavior or action that looks rewarding will make them consider trying it out for themselves. You have the ability to do so many great things and change lives in a positive way while you're currently living. Have an appetite for success and go claim prizes that are rightfully yours. You have what it takes to be a phenomenal person. You can accomplish anything you want in life as long as you continue to have a true appetite for success. If your appetite for success is real, you can't fail. People that are truly hungry for success eventually get rewarded after putting in blood, sweat, and tears. When your appetite for success is real and matches your consistent hard work, you're bound to enter into an exciting zone of winning. Being in a zone of winning is a great feeling. When you're winning, you may feel as if you're at the top of your game. When you're at the top of your game, you're completely unstoppable. Your appetite for success combined with hard work can take you places that may be seen by others as impossible destinations. Nothing is impossible when your appetite for success is like an inner burning flame that can't be easily put out. You're a champion no matter what anyone else may tell you. Just work your butt off to achieve greatness.

EXTREME MAKEOVER

When we can physically witness our lives operating in complete disarray or see ourselves behaving in a manner that's well short of our best, it's clearly time to begin the process of conducting an extreme makeover. As imperfect human beings, none of us are exempt from potentially falling short of being the phenomenal individuals we were created to be. When you're able to recognize that certain things about the way you live aren't right, it's a must that you begin making adjustments to your life. Change can be a very beautiful thing, especially when it's going to produce better results than what we're currently experiencing. Take a short pause in your life and take a look in the mirror. The fast pace world we currently live in does a great job with keeping most of us occupied with many things to do. As a result, we may forget to take time every so often to reflect on our personal well-being and behavior. When you look at the man in the mIrror, are you truly satisfied with what you see? Are you satisfied with your current actions and behavior you display on the daily basis? If that answer is no, then it's time for you to begin an extreme makeover. If your answer is yes and your life is not in a complete mess, there's still no way you're one hundred percent up to part in every area of your life. As an imperfect human being with many flaws, there will never be a time in your life when you'll have it all together. Many people that walk this earth truly believe that they're flawless and live a perfect life, but that's just a mere example of the level of stupidity people choose to embrace. Choose to embrace the true reality of your current actions and behavior. There may be room for improvement in your life to become a better friend, father, mother, or companion to someone else. Continuous improvement is what limitless growth is all about. Begin to conduct your extreme makeover and change your life forever.

During the process of undergoing an extreme makeover, one of the primary goals when making certain adjustments to our lives should be maintaining consistency with new changes that we implement. Maintaining consistency takes total dedication and a lot of hard work. It also requires for an individual to be completely locked in on the goal at hand. While on the journey and pursuit to maintain consistency, never forget that you're a human being. Relapse or briefly converting back to old behavior is possible for any human being. For example, many people who have a long history of substance abuse tend to relapse during their first attempt to get clean with rehab. This is very common for recovering substance abusers who continue to live or hangout in the same environment where their drug use took place. Even though they may convert back to abusing drugs after their initial attempt with rehab, they still have a chance to get back on track with getting clean. Just because you lose a battle doesn't mean you don't have a chance to win the war. We all lose battles every so often, which is a realistic human experience. Believing that a plan doesn't have the potential to get off track is not a realistic point of view. If you're a person who embodies this type of thinking, it's best that you take a different mental approach toward realistic possibilities that exist when making plans. Running into a road block or suffering a relapse in our actions can inflict a painful blow, but it never establishes that we're not able to bounce back. When phenomenal people fall on their back, they're able to dust themselves off and try again. You're still a phenomenal human being despite of your shortcomings. Having the confidence to conduct an extreme makeover shows that you have something great on the inside that wants to blossom on the outside. Never get discouraged if you fall short during your extreme makeover. Just get back focused on your goal and continue to grind hard for positive results.

While on the journey of conducting your extreme makeover, you may need help from other people along the way. In life, there are so many great things that we all are capable of doing without the assistance of other people, but the helping hand of another phenomenal person or group of people is a plus in any situation. During the process of trying to accomplish a goal, such as an extreme makeover, getting help from other people can cut down the amount of time it takes you to implement new changes into your life. During your time on this earth, you've had the pleasure of discovering that time is not on your side. There could be so many things you want to accomplish within a single day, but you may not be able to fulfil every single task because of the amount of time needed to complete every task. You're only given twenty-four hours within a single day just like everyone else that's currently living. Some goals can take up to weeks, months, and even years to complete. If you're able to get assistance from other people when accomplishing your goals, the timeframe it takes for you to claim victory may be cut in half. Never leave out receiving help from other people as an alternative for reaching your goals quicker. Besides helping you cut down the timeframe of implementing new positive changes into your life, the people that grind with you during your extreme makeover can also provide an extra boost of encouragement through the process. An extra boost of encouragement and support from positive people can be a big part of the winning formula for successfully conducting an extreme makeover. When you lack the discipline to consistently practice new behaviors on the regular basis, your helpers during your extreme makeover will be there to remind you that you're slacking and need to pick up your effort. True friends and real helpers never have a problem with telling you the truth. Whenever you feel that your extreme makeover is becoming too challenging for you, your helpers can be there to give you words of encourage to keep pressing forward.

Change can be a very challenging process for most of us. However, we all are capable of adjusting to change and thriving within new environmental conditions, new roles, or new actions. When it comes to conducting an extreme makeover, change is possible, especially for those who have the courage to believe. Believing that change is possible can allow you to focus less on the bumps in the road when you're traveling to your destination of completing an extreme makeover. If you're not able to win the mental battle of believing you can change, it becomes harder for you to produce strong efforts in the physical realm. Change interrupts the flow of common behavior patterns and instincts an individual may develop over a period of years. A great portion of the behavioral patterns and instincts that we all tend to learn are generally passed down to us from our family members. Behavioral patterns that are passed down from generation to generation are viewed as the norm within a particular family. This usually accounts for both positive and negative behavioral patterns. When a child witness their older family members lie to other people regularly, steal from other people, display regular acts of laziness, or show regular signs of self-doubt, they can be misled to believe that these actions are considered acceptable. People look up to their elders for guidance on how to live and survive in this world. When people are taught negative behaviors on how to live, an extreme makeover is necessary in order to live a better life. Although taking action to change and break free from negative behavioral patterns is challenging, it's never impossible to do. When you're in the process of conducting an extreme makeover, have faith in your ability to change in order to become a better version of yourself. Self-improvement is the goal and only positive change can allow you to reach that goal. Now is the time to view any current negative behaviors or actions as your old way of living. Allow change to carve and mold you into a unique form, smoothing out your rough edges like an artist would do when they're shaping a clay sculpture. Accept positive change and watch your life transform into greatness.

Behind your efforts of practicing positive change during an extreme makeover, you'll begin to see positive life changing results unfold in a slow progressive manner. It takes a great deal of both effort and time to witness visual signs of achieving positive life changing results, which could be compared to the feeling of running a marathon. Marathons can cover a great distance of multiple miles before reaching the finish line. In the beginning of a marathon, the finish line is not in direct view, but it becomes more visible as you steadily draw closer to it during the last stretch of the race. Also, as you get closer to the finish line during the final section of the marathon, the crowd that's watching the race from the sidelines begins to look as if it's steadily growing in size with every step you take. The crowd gets louder as you draw near the finish line, with many onlookers waiting to celebrate with runners as they cross the finish line. Getting to the finish line of a race takes time and tremendous effort. When making efforts to accomplish certain goals in life, some people fail to be patient and allow their hard work to slowly bring about positive results. We currently live in a very fast paced world where many people want their wishes to be answered right on the spot. In the midst of being impatient, many people choose to just completely give up on a goal because their efforts aren't producing results in the timeframe they predicted. Predictions and estimations can be great for drawing up positive outcomes, but they're never definite. Achieving greatness takes time and is not an easy task for any human being. Embracing this concept gives us the ability to stay level headed during our journey of completing a goal. During your extreme makeover, continue to keep putting in effort even if you haven't started seeing signs of positive change. Furthermore, it's always possible that positive change could actually be physically present within our lives and we just fail to catch it with the human eye. There's only so much that a human being can focus on at a particular time. The world we live in is extremely busy and many actions that take place around us during the day may not catch our attention. Have patience during your extreme makeover and just continue to keep putting forth effort. When the time is right, the signs of positive change will be more visible than ever.

UNDERDOG STATUS

Being in a position where you're classified as an underdog labels you as unfavorable to come out on top. Underdogs generally have limited resources and have to endure the lack of support from other people when they're trying to accomplish certain tasks. Even though underdogs are viewed as less favorable to do better than others, they still have a chance to prosper and become the best at what they do. Limited resources and lack of support from other people doesn't equal defeat. A true champion has the ability to overcome these challenges to claim victory. If you've been labeled or classified as an underdog by society, you still have a chance to be great and do phenomenal things in life. The only person on this earth that determines what you can accomplish and achieve in life is you. If you choose to believe any negative predictions that other people place over your life, you'll definitely hinder your growth. Your family history or current environment doesn't determine your future. Coming from a family that may have struggled financially for many years or many generations doesn't take away the possibility that you can achieve great wealth in your future. Growing up in a neighborhood that's extremely crime or drug infested cannot prohibit you from becoming a position role model and changing the lives of other people for the better. People with amazing talents can survive and make their way through the worst environmental conditions that life has to offer. Many of our ancestors who managed to accomplish great things in life had to deal with the adversity of being an underdog. As long as you believe in yourself, even when the odds are against you, you have a great chance to fight a good battle. When you're involved in a competition, you may be required to put in extra time and effort to get in a position where you can stand in the same class with other great achievers. Underdogs may not be on the same level as other individuals who are considered to be more superior, but they still have a chance to be crowned as a champion in the end.

For an underdog, limited resources are very often considered to be a normal existence. In life, some people are fortunate to have access to a multitude of available resources that can be extremely helpful. However, most people in this world have to combat the challenges they endure regularly with limited resources that provide little assistance. Even with the existence of limited resources, greatness can still be achieved by an underdog. As an underdog, you must do your best to squeeze every single ounce of energy and life out of the resources that are available to you. Always keep in mind that the availability of limited resources is far better than having no resources at your disposal. Having no resources to work with at all could be a complete nightmare. Take complete advantage of all the resources available to you, leaving nothing behind that could be used for your benefit. Along with using everything you can possibly get out of your available resources, put in an enormous amount of energy and effort into your actions. In your actions to capture greatness, go above and beyond the normal efforts of a typical or average human that has limitless resources to use. When classified as an underdog, if getting your day started earlier than other people gives you more time to do extra work, take advantage of waking up before the competition. You can't be lazy or be afraid to work harder if you really want to give yourself a chance at chasing greatness. In addition, working harder and going above and beyond in your efforts may expose you to new resources that were once not available to you. Discovering new resources is a blessing that will assist you with chasing goals.

When you're labeled as an underdog in the eyes of other people, be prepared to experience lack of support from others. In our society, people who are recognized as being the best at what they do professionally receives more public support than others in their field who are labeled as minor competition. For example, professional football and basketball teams that have won multiple championships or more championships than other teams in their sport have the biggest fan base. These popular championship teams are also sponsored by some of the biggest band names and companies in the world. The teams in professional sports that don't achieve much success or are rarely in the conversation of potentially winning a championship receive little support from the fans of their sport. They usually have a very small fan base, compared to other successful professional teams. In the business world, popular brands and products that are recognized as the best in the world attract the most supporters and customers. Their competitors, whose brands or products are not on the same level, struggle to maintain public support and obtain growth. This is the reason why we see so many businesses close permanently every single year. From a realistic perspective, who wouldn't want to use highly respected brands and products or support what's been recognized by many people as the best of the best? For the most part, people are heavily attracted to what they perceive to be the best of the best. People gravitate toward greatness and show little to no interest in anything that's less than the best. From this point of view, it's easy to understand how an underdog can come up short on getting support from other people in the world. Underdogs very often get overlooked because of the attention that top dogs attract. However, lack of support from other people can't keep an underdog from claiming success. An underdog must truly believe in their abilities and become comfortable with not having supporters on their side. If you're an underdog, don't allow the lack of support from other people to shake your confidence. Keep pressing forward and continue to be your own cheerleader. Continue to keep grinding until you get the results you're looking for. As long as you believe in yourself, anything is possible.

Along with lack of support from other people, underdogs also have to endure negativity from individuals who don't want to see them prosper. In this cruel world we live in, many people make it their personal business to do whatever they can to possibly destroy other people confidence. Have you ever experienced a moment in life where another person or a group of people spoke negative and unnecessary predictions over your life? If not, just continue to keep living and you're bound to experience it one day. It can be a challenge to not allow negativity from others to affect you if you don't train yourself on how to deal with negative people. On the regular basis, underdogs will experience unwanted negative remarks and comments from other people. In order to stay level headed and remain cool, underdogs must develop thick skin to sustain the negative blows that people will dish out. If you're not properly prepared to endure negativity from other people, certain negative words and comments by others will feel like a cut from a sharp razor blade. Negativity from other people is designed to throw you off of your game. Allowing negativity to grab too much of your attention makes achieving your goals more difficult. Whatever you choose to focus your attention on in life, that's where the majority of your energy and time will be consumed. As an underdog, you really don't have much energy or time to waste, especially given that you're already fighting from behind in your battle to obtain success. Use all of your energy and time wisely every single day. Stay focused on your goals and dreams, despite the negative predictions that other people make about your life. When you finally obtain success by accomplishing your goals, the people that spoke negative outcomes over your life will then not have much to talk about. Chase your dreams and silence the haters.

The life of an underdog can be very challenging. Limited resources and lack of support from others comes with the territory of being an underdog. Despite having to deal with these unwanted challenges, underdogs can still be victorious and become champions. If you're an underdog, allow other people low expectations of you to light a fire within you. That inner fire should push you to work harder on making your goals and dreams become a reality. You deserve to have the best that life has to offer, but that reward will only come with hard work. Your future is determined by your actions and what you choose to believe, not by what other people think of you. You have what it takes to be crowned a true champion. Within everything you strive to do in life, you must be your biggest advocate. Believe it or not, some people in the world will support underdogs because they can relate to the struggle that underdogs have to face. When you do have a few people in your corner that truly supports you, let that give you another reason to keep chasing your dreams and goals. Kick your daily efforts into overdrive like you have nothing to lose. For an underdog, the only way to go is up, especially if you're already at rock bottom. You may have a steep mountain to climb, but anything is possible as long as you believe in yourself.

OWN YOUR GREATNESS

When you were born into this world, you were destined to be a great person who's able to accomplish many extraordinary things in life. When you wake up every single day, the world gets an opportunity to be blessed by your presence. As you travel through your walk of life, make it a priority to live up to your true identity by owning your greatness. You must first believe in yourself to own your greatness. Believing in your ability to accomplish monumental goals in life will assist with your development and growth. Development and growth is a continuous process and you must aid that process with the mindset of a true champion. Regardless of any setbacks or difficulties you may encounter in your life, you must continue to believe in your abilities and strive for success. When other people choose to have negative opinions about your capability to do great things, choose to believe differently from their opinions. You were born to be great and no person on this earth has the power to change that at all. Your life is in your hands and it's up to you to decide what you're going to do with it. Are you going to pursue your goals and dreams or will you accept and believe the negative hype that others create about your potential? You only get one life to live, so make it count. There's nothing that can hold you back from owning your greatness and changing other people lives in a positive way. The blood of a true champion and survivor is running through your veins. You possess great strength that can overcome some of the toughest challenges that life has to offer. You're designed to be an unstoppable and powerful locomotive that keeps moving forward in life. If you ever get knocked down in life, you have the strength to get back up and keep moving forward. Never lose focus and forget who you are in life. You're a champion and greatness is upon you.

In order to own your greatness, you have to enhance your skills and talents. Enhancing your skills and talents requires practice on your part. Practicing on your craft will allow you to grow and mature in your line of work. Some of the world's greatest athletes, musicians, artists, dancers, and writers all practiced on their craft to become better at what they do. Many people in this world are naturally gifted with certain skills and talents, but they too must continuously practice on their craft to elevate their skill set. Never let any of your skills or talents go to waste. Certain skills and talents can open doors of opportunity that you may have never imagined. In addition to practice, discovering credible information that provides tips on improving your craft and actively applying that information to your actions will take your skills to a higher level. Enhancing your skills and talents may require for you to put in countless hours of practice. You may have to make personal sacrifices in your life to free up more time for practicing on your craft. This may involve things such as cutting back on watching television, spending less time hanging out with your friends, or reframing from oversleeping a lot when you've actually had an adequate amount of rest to prepare you for the next day. Time is very precious and we all must use our time wisely. As you begin to put more practice into your craft, visible evidence of improvement should start to slowly unravel over time. Are you willing to make sacrifices in life to own your greatness? Will you continuously practice on your craft to grow and mature? Everything in your life relies on you. Practice on your craft and you'll definitely own your greatness.

If you make regular consistent efforts to become an accurate representation of what you were truly created to be, you'll be on your way to owning your greatness. When thinking about the future, you may have used your imagination to form a picture in your mind of you successfully obtaining a major goal. In order to get to the point of actually bringing that image in your mind into existence, you have to first earn small wins. The goal that you so desperately seek to obtain is the ultimate big win, but you cannot get to the big win without earning small wins. Regular consistent efforts will put you in position to earn small wins. Let's compare a goal or dream you want to achieve to the game of baseball. In baseball, when a player gets an opportunity to step up to bat, the goal is to eventually score by making it back to home plate after hitting the ball and touching each base on the field. When players put points on the score board for their team, this is considered as a needed contribution toward helping the team win the game. Beating the opponent is the ultimate big win. Before a team can claim that big win, other small achievements are needed. As mentioned, one of those small achievements starts with players getting hits when they step up to bat. Some players have a greater chance of hitting a home run when they step up to bat than others. This is mainly because of their great strength, ability to guess certain pitches, and ability to time their swing perfectly to make a good connection with the ball. Hitting home runs are possible, but they can be very difficult to do. Furthermore, getting a single hit at the plate in major league baseball is a difficult task itself.

In major league baseball, the league's standard batting average generally ranges between twenty-five to twenty-seven percent. This is for players that average about three at bats per game. Players with batting averages above thirty percent are considered very good batters. It's rarely seen that a player would even come close to batting around forty percent for an entire regular season. These batting averages demonstrate the degree of difficulty that exists when players attempt to get a hit in baseball. When a player steps up to bat, simply making contact with the ball during a pitch is equivalent to a small achievement. That's a good start. Also, hitting the ball in fair territory is considered as another small achievement. If a player doesn't hit the ball in fair territory and at least make it to first base safely, they give themselves no chance to possibly get in position to score. When a player has successfully made it to first, second, or even third base after making a hit, they must make sure they don't get tagged out when one of their teammates are up to bat. During a baseball game, base runners generally take a couple steps away from their base in the direction of the next base in front of them. Pitchers often glance at base runners before they throw a pitch to batters, checking for a possible opportunity to tag base runners out who allow too much distance between themselves and the base they're occupying. Not getting tagged out and costing your team a potential scoring run is definitely a plus for the team. The collection of all these small achievements is often needed to score and reach the ultimate goal, which is to claim a big win for the team.

The principle of earning small achievements in order to capture big wins applies to life as well. To reach major milestones in our lives, we all must first focus on perfecting or achieving small. If you're a college student, the ultimate goal is to graduate with your degree or certification. To perfect or achieve small as a student, you should be primarily focused on passing the course that you're currently taking. Take it one class at a time. Conquer what you currently have in front of you at the moment. As an even more direct approach toward achieving small as a student, focus on passing one assignment at a time. As you study hard and do what's necessary to pass your assignments, you'll definitely be on your way to passing your current class. In all your efforts to accomplish big goals and dreams, don't underestimate the power of perfecting and achieving small. On many occasions, we all become so locked in on wanting to obtain big accomplishments that we pay no attention to obtaining the small milestones that build momentum toward capturing big accomplishments. Future success lies within your ability to obtain small wins. When you were a child, you had to first master the ability to crawl in order to move around on your own. Once you were able and had the strength to stand up on your own two feet, you had to master maintaining your balance in order to walk step by step. Once you were able to walk gracefully with complete control and balance, you then began to run so fast that your parents couldn't keep up with you. Perfect and achieve small in order to grab hold of the desires of your heart.

To aid you on your quest to own your greatness, you must think positive about your future to get positive results. In the world we live in, it's very easy to get pulled into developing a negative mentality about life. Our setbacks, failures, and disappointments can sometimes leave us feeling as if there's no hope for a brighter future. Encountering a loss has the potential to strike a mighty powerful blow to anyone's confidence and faith. Also, there are some people we come in contact with in life that always have negative things to say about life or us and may attempt to pass their negative energy off onto us. There are many things that can come against you on the daily basis, but do your absolute best to continue to think positive about your life. On many occasions, it can be very challenging to continue to think positive when it feels like the world around you is crumbling down on your head. On some days, you may even lose the battle of staying positive and hopeful about the future. There's nothing wrong with that. The most important thing to do in those situations is to not get stuck in a rut for too long or allow it to become a permanent way of life for you. When you experience setbacks or failures, take into consideration that those situations are just temporary and will eventually subside. Setbacks and failures are beneficial in that they allow us to discover certain faults in our approach toward accomplishing a goal. When you carefully address certain faults in your approach toward obtaining goals, making effective adjustments in how you carry out your efforts from that point on will give you a better chance of finally accomplishing your goals. Instead of making excuses in times of setbacks and failures, just make adjustments in your approach. Always think positive about your future because greater things are to come.

Your existence is a blessing to the entire world and the people that are around you on the daily basis. When you step into a room full of people, your presence alone will put a smile on many faces. As you speak words into existence and share your personal thoughts with others, people lives are changed forever. You have a unique ability to change people lives in a very positive way. Be a positive role model for others and show them that they shouldn't be afraid to own their greatness as well. Fear can hinder any individual from walking into their true destiny. Be an example for others in showing them that they too have what it takes to accomplish great things in life despite being an imperfect human being. Greatness will forever dwell within the boundaries of imperfection. The natural talents and skills you possess were given to you for the purpose of putting them to use, not for them to go to waste. Bless the world with the greatness you possess and you'll begin to achieve major accomplishments. Never be afraid to display your greatness and shine like a bright star in the midnight sky. Gravitate to new heights by continuously believing in your abilities and having the confidence of a true champion. Greatness is in your blood and that's something you can't deny. When you wake up every single day, believe that greatness is upon you.

LIMITLESS GROWTH

Throughout your walk of life, it's beneficial for you to be hungry for knowledge and grow as a person on a continuous basis. Limitless growth should be a way of life for all mankind. It must be embedded in our hearts and minds in order for us to become the best possible version of ourselves. For all adults, it's best that we instill the mindset of limitless growth into the youth who will one day be looked upon as role models and leaders. Our younger generation will one day occupy certain positions and roles in society that will require them to make decisions that affect others. With the existence of so many tragic events that have occurred in our history, our world is in desperate need of more good leaders and role models. Currently, there's a huge shortage of good leaders and role models in our society. If we had more good leaders and role models, the world would be a better place. The practice of limitless growth is a great starting point for becoming a good leader and role model that can make positive contributions to this world. Choose to make limitless growth a part of your life. Every single day you wake up and get another opportunity to experience the beauty of life, self-improvement should be one of the top priorities on your agenda. Limitless growth is a necessity that's just as important as food and sleep. Being that we're all imperfect human beings, it's certain that there will always be particular areas in our lives we can greatly improve on. Do you truly understand how powerful you are and what you're able to achieve during your lifetime? Establish a mindset of limitless growth and take your life to new heights. Everything that you're capable of accomplishing in life is riding on your efforts and daily decision making.

Choosing to take a stand and make limitless growth a way of life starting today will begin to change the world around you. Practicing limitless growth requires for an individual to be brutally honest with themselves when conducting a self-assessment. Conducting a self-assessment involves analyzing your actions and decision making. For the most part, you're already consciously aware of certain areas of your life that needs improvement. At times, you may tend to purposely overlook certain troubled areas of your life that needs great attention. Many of us do this on a regular basis. When conducting a self-assessment, be honest in your efforts of determining and pointing out what you can improve on as a person. Areas of improvement may include your overall personal attitude, the way you treat other people, or the way you make decisions. You should never be ashamed of the areas in your life that need improvement. All human beings lack perfection. Take action by making efforts to improve those areas immediately. The sooner you start the process of making adjustments to your life, the better off your future will turn out. As you begin to strive toward making improvements in certain areas of your life, the world you see before your eyes will start to look a little different. You'll begin to build momentum toward getting your life on a path destined for greatness. When you begin to practice limitless growth, certain doors of opportunity that were once not present may begin to appear in your life. Wise decision making changes situations. Practice limitless growth on the regular basis and always encourage others to do the same.

During your journey through life, be confident that you have what it takes to learn and grow as a person every single day. Before you begin to build relationships with other people to get to know them personally, make a vow to get to know yourself first. Discover all of your strengths and weaknesses. Discover your true desires in life and find your way to live life to the fullest. If you're an empty cup yourself, there's absolutely no way you can pour into others. Help and improve on yourself first before you reach out to assist others. Be confident that you can greatly improve on your current weaknesses. Never indulge in mediocrity by believing that your current weaknesses will forever hold you down. You have the power to overcome any weaknesses because you were born to be a conqueror. If you go through life believing that you can't overcome your weaknesses, you won't. By believing that, you would have already lost the first round of the fight within the mental battle. Having belief in your abilities is everything. All human beings have the ability and strength to improve their weaknesses no matter how bad they may appear to look. No matter how high the mountain may be for you to climb and overcome, you can do it. You were always meant to blossom and grow stronger as you go through life. Some of life challenges may have left you with bruises and forced you to encounter setbacks, but you're currently still breathing and moving forward in life. Envision challenges as an opportunity to learn and push you to become a better person.

Live your best life by practicing limitless growth. You still have more great things to accomplish in life. You still have more people to make laugh and smile. There are still more people that need your help, guidance, and love. Your presence is still needed at certain places and events to get things done effectively. Your overall existence is still important to this world. You make things happen and you make life better for other people. You still have more challenges to overcome that will show your greatness. Enjoy every moment of your life and continue to grow while you're at it. As you continue to practice limitless growth, you'll amaze other people and give them courage to try it themselves. Put your foot down and set the standards for your life. You're victorious and greatness will forever be a part of you. Have confidence in yourself at all times, even when life throws you unwanted curveballs. Stand tall and always continue to keep pressing forward in life. When you have confidence and believe in yourself, you're unstoppable. Take charge of your life and walk into your destiny. Never stop growing.